# SONGS OF '76

*Washington's reception at Trenton*

# Songs of '76

## A Folksinger's History
### OF THE
### REVOLUTION

by Oscar Brand

PUBLISHED BY
M. EVANS AND COMPANY, INC., NEW YORK

M. Evans and Company titles are distributed in
the United States by the J. B. Lippincott Company,
East Washington Square, Philadelphia, Pa. 19105,
and in Canada by McClelland & Stewart, Ltd.,
25 Hollinger Road, Toronto, M4B 3G2, Ontario

Library of Congress Catalog Card Number: 72-83733
ISBN 0-87131-092-9 (Cloth)
ISBN 0-87131-170-4 (Paper)
*Design by Ronald Farber*
Manufactured in the United States of America

9 8 7 6 5 4 3 2

ACKNOWLEDGEMENT

*I feel it important to thank Herbert Katz for his editorial guidance, and Douglas Townsend for his musical advice.*

# Contents

[ x ]

# Introduction

I've been singing since I was five years old. Some of the songs I learned as a boy in Manitoba told of places I'd never heard of, of passions that were almost incomprehensible. When I came to study history in school, I found that my view of history wasn't the same as that of the other children. They were learning dates while I was learning people. Their General Wolfe was a stick-figure, mine was a romantic lover mourned by a beautiful English lady. Their Louis Riel was a cartoon badman trying to overturn the lawful government of Canada. My Louis Riel was a passionate Metis, dark, handsome, and graceful. I knew it was true because the ballads said so.

Among my favorites were songs written by Loyalists who had fled the United States after the American Revolution. When I came to the United States, I learned that there was another side to the story. I began hearing songs that cursed the vile Tories who had remained faithful to the Empire. Again I found that many of the songs spoke of people and issues of which I knew very little.

After a while my curiosity drove me to books about the Revolution, and to further collections of songs. I perceived strange stories in these antique accounts and marvelously interesting sidelights. Some of these I considered more vital than the standard accounts of historical chronology. I noted them down and shared them with my audiences, on television, radio, or in concert.

That's how I came to write this book. That's why it's a "folksinger's history." It's my eyewitness report of events that have paraded before my mind's eye. If I slight an important general and raise some feeble figure to towering stature, it's because the second touched me and the first did not. If I have given only one paragraph to a decisive battle and a page to a minor skirmish, it's because the skirmish remained in my memory when the decisive battle had faded into the past.

You see, singers are eyewitnesses. We tell our stories in the first person and wander through the ancient melodies as if they were our natural homes. We are the heroes of the happy songs and the tragic figures of the sad ballads. We are partisan where a historian would be dispassionate. When "I" am a Tory, I sneer at the wretched colonials, when "I" am a Rebel, I curse the cowardly thieves who try to steal my Revolution.

Give your voice to the melodies and your mind to the tales of Rebellion and Reaction, and perhaps you'll enjoy them as much as I have enjoyed them, and even believe them as much as I believe them. Because as far as I'm concerned, my Revolution beats them all.

# The Songs

MANY OF the songs and quotations have been collected from old manuscripts. Very often, there is no indication of the music which once accompanied the words. Sometimes, the printed broadsides mention an "air" which would fit the lyrics. Sometimes that "air" has been long forgotten, or so changed by time that it no longer fits the material.

For that reason I have often set the words to tunes which I believe are appropriate, and in the original style. In some cases, the songs are "jury" versions—verses and melodies selected and arranged from the many variants available. I hope this will not interfere with their original intent. It is important that, as much as is possible, we hear the story of the American Revolution in the words of the people who inhabited it.

*Reading the Stamp Act in Boston*

IN 1765 George III of England, King of a world wide empire, found the national debt to be rising uncontrollably. Seeking creative new ways of raising the money, George and his advisers decided that the prosperous American colonies should help bear the cost of their own defense, as well as help defray the expenses of England's years of continental wars. England had been supporting a large standing army in the American West and Canada to protect the borders from Indians. Certainly, they reasoned, the colonists would be happy to help pay the salaries of the troops.

With this in mind, in 1765 Parliament passed the Stamp Act, taxing legal documents, dice, playing cards, licenses, ships papers, ballad broadsides, pamphlets, and newspapers. It would have been wiser had they exempted the pamphlets, balladeers, and newspapers, for these began an inflammatory campaign, at first against the Stamp Act, and finally, against the tyranny of "Foreign Domination."

The pamphleteer-balladeer who wrote "American Taxation," Peter St. John, was also a schoolmaster in Norwalk, Connecticut. From the day when the news of the Stamp Act first arrived aboard the ship *Edward* on April 8, 1765, he began a musical campaign against the tax, joining with the angry newspapers which declared, "There is no way to elude the design of it but by rejecting the whole as an unconstitutional attempt upon our liberties."

*Colonists denouncing the Stamp Act*

[ 3 ]

# American Taxation

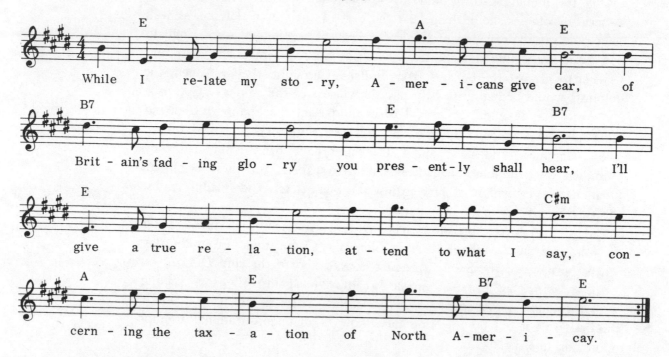

While I re-late my sto - ry, A - mer - i - cans give ear, of Brit - ain's fad - ing glo - ry you pres - ent-ly shall hear, I'll give a true re - la - tion, at - tend to what I say, con - cern - ing the tax - a - tion of North A - mer - i - cay.

While I relate my story, Americans give ear,
Of Britain's fading glory you presently shall hear,
I'll give a true relation, attend to what I say,
Concerning the taxation of North Americay.

The cruel lords of Britain who glory in their shame,
The project they have hit on they joyfully proclaim,
Tis what they're striving after, our right to take away,
And rob us of our charter in North Americay.

There are two mighty Speakers who rule in Parliament,
Who ever have been seeking some mischief to invent,
'Twas North and Bute, his father, the horrid plan did lay,
A mighty tax to gather in North Americay.

These subtle arch-combiners addressed the British court,
With Satan undersigners of this obscure report,
There is a pleasant landscape that lieth far away,
Beyond the wide Atlantic in North Americay.

There is a wealthy people who sojourn in that land,
Their churches all with steeples most delicately stand,
Their houses like the gilly are painted red and gay,
They flourish like the lily in North Americay.

Their land with milk and honey continually doth flow,
The want of food or money they seldom ever know,
They heap up golden treasure, they have no debts to pay,
They spend their time in pleasure in North Americay.

New music and edited text © 1972 by Oscar Brand

[ 4 ]

With gold and silver laces they do themselves
    adorn,
The rubies deck their faces refulgent as the
    morn,
With sparkle in their glasses they spend each
    happy day,
In merriment and dances in North Americay.

O King, you've heard the sequel of what we
    now subscribe,
Is it not just and equal to take this wealthy
    tribe?
The question being askéd, His Majesty did say,
"My subjects shall be taxéd in North Ameri-
    cay."

Invested with a warrant my publicans shall go,
The tenth of all their current they surely shall
    bestow,
I will forbear to flatter, I'll rule the mighty
    sway,
I'll take away the charter from North Americay.

O George! you are distracted, you'll by ex-
    perience find,
The laws you have enacted are of the blackest
    kind,
I'll make a short digression and tell you by the
    way,
We fear not your oppression in North Ameri-
    cay.

Our fathers were distresséd while in their na-
    tive land,
By tyrants were oppresséd as we do under-
    stand,
For freedom and religion they were resolved
    to stray,
And trace the desert regions of North Ameri-
    cay.

We are their bold descendants, for liberty we'll
    fight,
The claim to independence we challenge as our
    right,
'Tis what kind Heaven gave us, who can it
    take away?
O, Heaven sure will save us in North Americay.

*A tax collector challenged*

THE COLONIES were not alone in objecting to the Stamp Tax. English merchants were noisy in their opposition, many of them afraid that they would not be able to recover their investments in the New World. King George, in fact, was astonished to find "subjects capable of encouraging the rebellious disposition which unhappily exists in some of my colonies in America."

George William Frederick, King of England, was, at first, a very popular monarch. He was a solid example of domestic virtue, in charming contrast to his father and grandfather. He sincerely believed that his grandfather's advisers had led the country to near ruin, and he replaced William Pitt as chief minister with John Stuart, Lord Bute. Unfortunately, Lord Bute's sole qualification was that he had once been the King's tutor, and he was supplanted by George Grenville, his chancellor of the exchequer.

It was Grenville who proposed the Stamp Tax and he became immediately the prime target for vilification in England and the colonies. He was accused of ruining colonial commerce and of causing the suspension of many newspapers. Grenville was blamed, for instance, when *The Philadelphia Journal* black-bordered the following announcement on its front page:

> I am sorry to be obliged to acquaint my readers that as the STAMP ACT is feared to be obligatory upon us after the first of November ensuing (the fatal Tomorrow), the Publisher of this Paper, unable to bear the burthen, has thought it expedient to stop a while in order to deliberate whether any Methods can be found to elude the chains forged for us . . .

The Stamp Act didn't bring in very much money—the ancient tradition of smuggling and tax evasion was too deeply engrained in the colonies. However the Act did make such radicals as Samuel Adams and Patrick Henry more popular and it helped create hundreds of musical protests such as "Granny Wales."

The song was published in 1823 by an "Old Revolutionary Soldier" who declared, "The author is a clear North American; one of the followers of Gen. GEORGE WASHINGTON. The privations he has undergone has taught him that pure INDEPENDENCE is worth something."

# Granny Wales

As Gran-ny a-rose in the morn-ing so soon, she put on her
pet-ti-coat, a-pron, and gown, "I've ver-y bad news that last
night came to me, They're wrong-ing my chil-dren far o-ver the sea."

Scene 1

As Granny arose in the morning so soon,
She put on her petticoat, apron, and gown;
"I've very bad news that last night came to me,
They're wronging my children far over the
    sea."

Scene 2

Then Granny Wales mounted her horse in a
    rage,
And straight up to London it was her next
    stage,
As she was a-riding up through London street,
'Twas there my Lord Grenville and Bute she
    did meet.

She said, "Noble gentlemen, tell me the facts,
Are you the ringleaders of this new tax?
To enslave my sons that's in a foreign land,
You are the two villains as I understand."

"Oh no, my dear Granny, you're wrongly in-
    formed,
To enslave America we don't intend,
But this land is our King's, we do solemnly say,
And we will make the laws for your sons to
    obey."

Scene 3

"It's a lie, it's a lie!" said Old Granny in haste,
"For it's very well known from the east to the
    west,
That they ventured their lives at the price of
    their blood,
But with taxes you cover their land like a
    flood."

New music and edited text © 1972 by Oscar Brand

THE STAMP Act was so unpopular that the King was forced to dismiss its author, Lord Grenville. His successor, Lord Rockingham, then repealed the Act. However, the King insisted that a Declaratory Act be passed, stating the right of Britain to tax its colonies. This was also unpopular, and Lord Rockingham was dismissed. The King then turned, probably with some distaste, to the man he had accused of helping ruin England, William Pitt, now Earl of Chatham.

But Pitt was ill, in mind and in body, and his Chancellor of the Exchequer, Charles Townshend, took over the reins of government. In 1767, Townshend introduced a Bill imposing duties on American imports of paper, glass, lead, and tea. America began an angry boycott of British goods. The "Sons of Liberty" began to travel about, nailing up posters which named merchants who dared trade in taxed merchandise:

"It is desired that the Sons and Daughters of Liberty would not buy any one thing of him, for in so doing, they will bring disgrace upon themselves and their posterity for ever and ever. Amen." This doesn't mean that everyone had turned revolutionary. John Adams stated that a very influential third of the colonials were Loyal to the Crown. But they were ill-served by an insensitive Parliament and the King.

Benjamin Franklin wrote to a Scottish friend: "Every man in England seems to consider himself as a piece of a sovereign over America; seems to jostle himself into the throne with the King, and talks of 'our subjects in the Colonies' . . . And yet, there remains among that people so much respect, veneration, and affection for Britain, that, if cultivated prudently, with kind usage and tenderness for their privileges, they might be easily governed still for ages without force, or any considerable expense. But I do not see here a sufficient quantity of the wisdom that is necessary to produce such a conduct, and I lament the want of it."

In Pennsylvania, a gentle lawyer of conservative persuasion, John Dickinson, wrote a series of "Letters From a Farmer," in which he prayed for a happy ending to the squabble: "We have an excellent prince, in whose good dispositions towards us we may confide. We have a generous, sensible and humane nation, to whom we may apply."

Dickinson kept hoping for peace, even refusing to sign the Declaration of Independence when he later became a member of the Congress. But he never temporized in his rejection of the British power to tax the colonies. In 1768, he sent the following note to James Otis of Massachusetts: "I enclose you a song for American freedom. I have long renounced poetry, but, as indifferent songs are very powerful on certain occasions, I venture to invoke the deserted muses."

The song was published in the *Boston Gazette* on July 18, 1768, and it became one of New England's favorite revolutionary anthems.

# In Freedom We're Born

Come, join hand in hand, brave A-mer-i-cans all, And
rouse your bold hearts at fair Lib-er-ty's call. No___ tyr-an-nous acts shall suppress your just claim, Nor stain with dis-hon-or A-mer-i-ca's name. In
free-dom we're born and in free-dom we'll live. Our purs-es are read-y,
Stead-y, friends, stead-y, Not as slaves,___but as free men our mon-ey we'll give.

Come join hand in hand, brave Americans all,
And rouse your bold hearts at fair Liberty's
  call,
No tyrannous acts shall suppress your just
  claim,
Nor stain with dishonor America's name,
CHORUS:
  In freedom we're born and in freedom we'll
    live,
  Our purses are ready,
  Steady, friends, steady,
  Not as slaves, but as freemen our money
    we'll give.

How sweet are the labors that freemen endure,
That they shall enjoy all the profit, secure,
No more such sweet labors Americans know,
If Britons shall reap what Americans sow.
  CHORUS:

Then join hand in hand, brave Americans all,
By uniting we stand, by dividing we fall,
In so righteous a cause let us hope to succeed,
For Heaven approves of each generous deed.
                                    CHORUS:

This bumper I crown for our sovereign's health,
And this for Britannia's glory and wealth,
That wealth, and that glory immortal may be,
If she is but just, and we are but free. CHORUS:

New music and edited text © 1957 by Oscar Brand

AFTER THE Townshend Acts, mobs began to terrorize the collectors and manhandle the King's officers. Even distinguished citizens, disguised as workmen, went about with buckets of tar and bags of feathers, which they applied to the bare skins of Loyalist merchants and customs officials. A mob in New York burned the coach of the Lieutenant Governor and tore down the house of the local military commandant. A stamp officer in South Carolina reported that an angry group of rebellious citizens included thinly disguised relatives, friends, and business associates.

The newspapers printed attack after attack against the King's representatives, but spared the King himself. One couplet addressed to George Grenville, who had authored the Stamp Tax, read:

> To make us all Slaves, now you've lost, Sir! the Hope,
> You've but to go hang yourself. We'll find the Rope.

Disobedience became the fashion, resisting the law became a patriotic duty. John Hancock, for instance, one of the richest merchants in Boston, was an expert in contraband and smuggled goods. Of course, he had always kept his illicit activities secret. However, when a curious group of Royal Customs Officials boarded his ship, *The Liberty*, intending to confiscate its illegal cargo of wine, he openly led a party of colonists in a sortie which sent the Crown officials swimming for shore.

Where violence is currency, fear is a commonplace. Even after the repeal of the Stamp Act, the mobs continued their intimidation, as if they were merely social clubs or debating groups. Public debate was stifled, and Loyalists began to confine their arguments to anonymous letters-to-the-editor. Soon after John Dickinson's "In Freedom We're Born" was printed, the *Boston Gazette* received an answer to it. The prudent writer refused to sign his name, but the editors demonstrated a notable adherence to the principles of free expression. They printed the song, "Come Shake your Dull Noodles," a parody on "In Freedom We're Born".

# Come Shake Your Dull Noodles

(SEE *"In Freedom We're Born"* FOR THE MUSIC)

Come shake your dull noodles, ye pumpkins,
  and bawl,
And own that you're mad at fair Liberty's call,
No scandalous conduct can add to your shame,
Comdemn'd to dishonor, inherit the fame.
CHORUS:
  In folly you're born and in folly you'll live,
  To madness still ready,
  And stupidly steady,
  Not as men, but as monkeys, the tokens you
    give.

Such villains, such rascals all dangers despise,
And stick not at mobbing when mischief's the
prize,
But short is your harvest, nor long shall you
  know,
The pleasure of reaping what other men sow.
                  CHORUS:

All ages shall speak with contempt and amaze,
Of the vilest banditti that swarm'd in these
  days,
In defiance of halters, of whips and of chains,
The rogues would run riot, fools for their pains.
                  CHORUS:

Gulp down your last dram, for the gallows
  now groans,
And, overdepress'd, her lost empire bemoans,
While we quite transported and happy shall be,
From mobs, knaves and villains, protected and
  free.
                  CHORUS:

New music and edited text © 1957 by Oscar Brand

*A Loyalist tarred and feathered*

[ 11 ]

HOW WAS it possible for such strangely assorted colonies filled with wildly disparate individuals to achieve any sort of unity? Land-owners felt that trade should be taxed. Tradesmen felt that land should be taxed. They finally reached an agreement that there should be no taxes at all, certainly none without representation. King George and his advisers considered this a ridiculous demand. Weren't the colonials represented in Parliament? Didn't English businessmen represent the tradespeople adequately, and weren't there plenty of radical Englishmen siding with the colonies in every dispute?

In fact, the title "Sons of Liberty" had been bestowed on the mobs by a member of Parliament. Colonel Isaac Barré had been wounded in the Battle of Quebec, and knew well the free spirit of the American colonials. In direct debate with Charles Townshend, author of the new Revenue Acts, Barré declaimed:

> Your oppressions planted them in America. . . . They fled from your tyranny. . . . They grew up by your neglect of them. . . . They have nobly taken arms in your defence. . . . You sent, to spy out their liberties, to misrepresent their actions, and to prey upon them, men whose behavior on many occasions has caused the blood of those sons of Liberty to recoil within them.

Another very clear expression of sympathy with the angry colonials was published in the *St. James Chronicle* in London. It was an answer to the preceding parody on "In Freedom We're Born." This parody of a parody was sung, as were its two predecessors, to the melody of a song which was originally written to extol the virtues of the British Navy, "Hearts Of Oak."

# Come Swallow Your Bumpers

(SEE *"In Freedom We're Born"* FOR THE MUSIC)

Come swallow your bumpers, ye Tories, and
roar,
That the sons of fair Freedom are hamper'd
once more,
But know that no cutthroats our spirits can
tame,
Nor a host of oppressors shall smother the
flame.
CHORUS:
   In freedom we're born, and like sons of the
    brave,
   We'll never surrender,
   But swear to defend her,
   And scorn to survive if unable to save.

Our wives and our babes, still protected, shall
know,
Those who dare to be free, shall for ever be so,
On these arms and these hearts they may safely
rely,
For in freedom we'll live and like heroes we'll
die. CHORUS:

New music and edited text © 1957 by Oscar Brand

Ye insolent tyrants! who wish to enthrall,
Ye minions, ye placemen, pimps, pensioners all,
How short is your triumph! how feeble your
trust!
Your honors must wither and nod to the dust.
CHORUS:

When oppress'd and reproach'd, our king we
implore,
Still firmly persuaded our rights he'll restore,
When our hearts beat to arms, to defend a just
right,
Our monarch rules there and forbids us to fight.
CHORUS:

*King George III*

THERE ARE many who believe that a young William Pitt could've prevented the violent Civil War. But there was no young William Pitt in 1767. "The Great Commoner" was old, tired, and ill. Worse still, he wasn't even "The Great Commoner," having allowed the King to honor him with the title "Earl of Chatham." He also allowed the King to use his name as Prime Minister of England while Townshend was, in truth, preparing the unpopular Acts.

By 1768 Pitt was even sicker, and resigned his office to the Duke of Grafton, Augustus Henry Fitzroy. Nevertheless, he was still considered "The supporter of Liberty and the terror of tyrants." When British merchants petitioned Parliament for repeal of the Stamp Act, Pitt announced that he "never had greater satisfaction than in the repeal of this Act."

By 1769 British exports to the colonies had fallen by one-half. The Parliament, by a tight majority of one vote agreed to suspend the duties immediately. However, they did feel that some minor tax should be kept on, just to show that they had the authority. They cleverly decided to maintain a harmless tax of three pence a pound on tea.

This decision made, the moderates in England and America sat back happily, expecting to enjoy the benefits of peace and prosperity. In 1767 the following song was published in London's *Gentlemen's Gazette* announcing the reconciliation of England, old Goody Bull, and her loving but contentious offspring, America. From force of habit, the credit for this magnificent stroke of diplomacy was accorded to William Pitt, the Earl of Chatham.

# Goody Bull

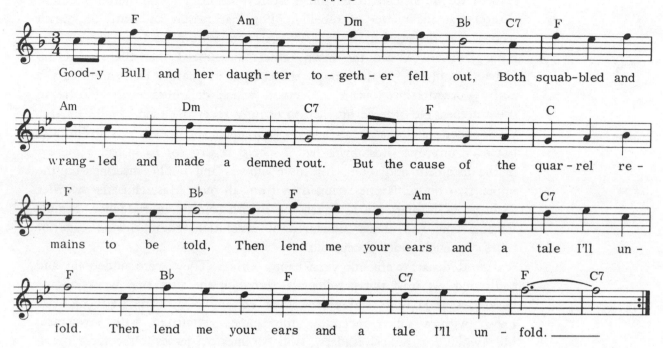

Good-y Bull and her daugh-ter to-geth-er fell out, Both squab-bled and wrang-led and made a demned rout. But the cause of the quar-rel re-mains to be told, Then lend me your ears and a tale I'll un-fold. Then lend me your ears and a tale I'll un-fold.

Goody Bull and her daughter together fell out,
Both squabbled, and wrangled and made a
   demned rout,
But the cause of the quarrel remains to be told,
Then lend me your ears and a tale I'll unfold.

*Scene 1*

The old lady, it seems, took a freak in her head,
That her daughter, grown woman, might earn
   her own bread,
The daughter was sulky and wouldn't come to,
And pray, what in this case can old women do?

In vain did the matron hold forth in the cause,
That the young one was able; her duty, the
   laws;

*Scene 2*

Ingratitude vile, disobedience far worse;
But she might e'en as well sung psalms to a
   horse.

Zounds, neighbor! quoth Pitt, what the devil's
   the matter?
A man cannot rest in his house for your clatter, *Scene 3*
Now, Goody, what ails you? Wake! woman,
   I say;
I am come to make peace in this desperate fray.

Be ruled by your friends, kneel down and ask *Scene 4*
   pardon,
You'd be sorry, I'm sure, should she walk Co-
   vent Garden,
Alas! Cries the old woman, must I comply?
Well, I'd rather submit than the huzzy should
   die.

Come kiss the poor child, Pitt declares, and be
   friends,
Come and kiss your poor daughter, and make *Scene 5*
   her amends,
No thanks to you, mother; the daughter replied,
But thanks to my friend here, I've humbled
   your pride.

New music and edited text © 1972 by Oscar Brand

[ 15 ]

ALTHOUGH THERE had been plenty of incidents featuring tar and feathers and flouting of authority in every colony, Massachusetts seemed to the British to be the most revolutionary. And without doubt, Boston was the center of rebellion. For that reason an army of British troops was dispatched in 1768 to garrison Boston and to protect the King's officers. When the town fathers announced that there were no quarters available for the troops, the colonel in charge, Dalrymple of the 29th Worcestershires, made a decision which delighted every fanatic in the colonies. He ordered his men to occupy revered Faneuil Hall.

Faneuil Hall wasn't an ancient monument or a religious institution, but even improper Bostonians had a special regard for it. It had a market in the basement and rooms for town officers and public meetings on the upper two floors. Rustics tripped in from all over Massachusetts in order to boast of having seen it. With the British soldiers in residence, Samuel Adams, who had almost despaired of revolution, found his message of rebellion much more acceptable.

The Redcoats were not very happy either. They were underpaid and badly fed. At least thirty soldiers deserted in the first two weeks. Some hired out as laborers and cursed their employers as benighted colonials. Faced with a sullen reception, the soldiers retaliated with arrogance. Meanwhile the radical leaders, Will Molineaux, James Otis, Dr. Joseph Warren, John Hancock, and Samuel Adams, were spreading rumors of the dastardly activities of the "lobsters."

The first task in arranging a war is the defacing of the opposition. The enemy must be dehumanized. John Adams observed that this process had begun and there was an active, intentional effort of propaganda promoted by "certain busy characters," endeavoring "to enkindle an immortal hatred."

To the soldiers, the colonials were wretched and ungrateful, discontents and Rebels all. As this song demonstrates, the Redcoat was human, British, and probably homesick. It further demonstrates that he took some of his songs home with him, because I found it in a west country collection in the British Museum.

# The Wicked Rebels

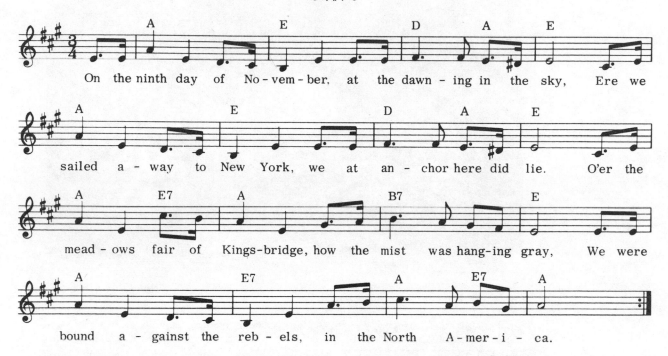

On the ninth day of No-vem-ber, at the dawn-ing in the sky, Ere we sailed a-way to New York, we at an-chor here did lie. O'er the mead-ows fair of Kings-bridge, how the mist was hang-ing gray, We were bound a-gainst the reb-els, in the North A-mer-i-ca.

On the ninth day of November at the dawning
    in the sky,
Ere we sailed away to New York, we at anchor
    here did lie,
O'er the meadows fair of Kingsbridge, how the
    mist was hanging gray,
We were bound against the Rebels in the North
    Americay.

Oh, how mournful was the parting of the
    soldiers and their wives,
For that no one knew for sartin they'd return
    home with their lives,
All the women were a-weeping and they cursed
    the cruel day,
That we sailed against the Rebels in the North
    Americay.

All the little babes were holding out their arms
    with saddest cries,
And the bitter tears were falling from their
    pretty simple eyes,
That their scarlet-coated daddies must be has-
    tening away,
For to fight the wicked Rebels in the North
    Americay.

Now with "God preserve our monarch" let us
    finish up our strain,
Be his subjects ever loyal and his honor all
    maintain,
May the Lord our voyage prosper and our
    arms across the sea,
And put down the wicked Rebels in the
    North Americay.

New music and edited text © 1957 by Oscar Brand

*The Boston Massacre*

HATRED BETWEEN British soldiers and colonists became more open and on the evening of March 5, 1770, the inevitable occurred. The *Boston Chronicle* printed the following story on March 8:

> Last Monday about 9 o'clock at night a most unfortunate affair happened in King Street. The sentinel posted at the Custom House, being surrounded by a number of people, called to the main-guard, upon which Captain Preston, with a party, went to his assistance, soon after which some of the party fired, by which the following persons were killed. Samuel Gray, rope maker, a mulatto man, named Attucks, and Mr. James Caldwell. . . .

The Town of Boston proceeded to collect depositions from witnesses who agreed generally on the following history: on the afternoon of March 2, a British soldier quarreled with one of the workmen at a rope-walk near his barracks. He challenged the workman to a fair fight, was beaten, and returned to his barracks for reinforcements. The new group was beaten off, and they went back to the barracks for more soldiers. More workman appeared and, in a while, a major struggle ensued. There was no victor, but the original workman was fired to pacify the angry soldiers. Nevertheless, their comrades promised to revenge the insults to the honor of the regiment.

A few days later—the evening of March 5—a dozen or more soldiers roistered through the town, armed with swords and cutlasses, and abused and assaulted citizens in their path, calling, "Where are the boogers! where are the cowards!" As they headed toward King Street, the meeting house bell was rung. People began to gather in King Street where a sentry was on guard near the Custom House. Some rowdies in the crowd, after a few angry words, began to throw snowballs at the sentry and he called for help.

The officer on guard was Captain Preston. Upon observing the angry mood of the crowd, he called out seven or eight soldiers to guard the Custom House. These men were of the 29th Regiment, the same regiment that had sworn vengeance on the townspeople. The soldiers, forced back by the mob, raised their muskets. It is said that Captain Preston shouted, "Don't fire! Don't fire!" But the soldiers claimed they heard only the word "fire," according to the *Chronicle*, which reported:

"Mr. Samuel Gray, killed on the spot by a ball entering his head.

"Crispus Attucks, a mulatto, killed on the spot, two balls entering his breast.

"Mr. James Caldwell, killed on the spot, by two balls entering his back.

"Mr. Samuel Maverick, a youth of seventeen years of age, mortally wounded; he died the next morning.

"Mr. Patrick Carr mortally wounded; he died the 14th instant.

"Christopher Monk and John Clark, youths about seventeen years of age, dangerously wounded. It is apprehended they will die.

"Mr. Edward Payne, merchant, standing at his door; wounded.

"Messrs. John Green, Robert Patterson, and David Parker; all dangerously wounded."

Hastily, but with great skill, Paul Revere engraved an incendiary picture of the Boston Massacre. The picture carried the following verses, written by Revere.

# The Boston Massacre

Un - hap - py Bos - ton, see thy sons de - plore, _____ Thy

hal - lowed walks be - smear'd with guilt - less gore, _____ While

faith - less Pres - ton and his sav - age bands, _____ With

mur - d'rous ran - cor stretch their blood - y hands. _____ Like

fierce bar - bar - ians grin - ning o'er their prey, _____ Ap -

prove the car - nage and en - joy the day. _____

Unhappy Boston, see thy sons deplore,
Thy hallowed walks besmear'd with guiltless gore,
While faithless Preston and his savage bands,
With murderous rancor stretch their bloody hands.
Like fierce barbarians grinning o'er their prey,
Approve the carnage and enjoy the day.

If scalding drops, from rage, from anguish wrung,
If speechless sorrows lab'ring for a tongue,
Or if a weeping world can aught appease,
The plaintive ghosts of victims such as these,
The Patriot's copious tears for each are shed,
A glorious tribute that embalms the dead.

New music and edited text © 1972 by Oscar Brand

But know, Fate summons to that awful goal,
Where justice strips the murderer of his soul,
Should venal courts, the scandal of the land,
Snatch the relentless villain from her hand,
Keen execrations on this plate inscrib'd,
Shall reach a judge who never can be bribed.

---

FOLLOWING THE Boston Massacre in 1770, Captain Preston and eight of his soldiers were remanded for trial for firing on civilians, and the two British regiments were ordered out of Boston to a barracks on Castle Island. But the damage had been done—the Massacre had given the Rebels new martyrs for their cause. Who would dare defend the murderers? Captain Preston, with remarkable wisdom, turned for help to a pair of well-known "Rebels," John Adams and Josiah Quincy, Jr. It's generally believed that some of Boston's leading radicals, including John Hancock, Joseph Warren, and Samuel Adams, thought it was a good idea to take the case. Perhaps they hoped to show that these Redcoats were being cast as scapegoats for higher-ups in the British Government.

For many, however, defending the men who perpetrated the Massacre was indefensible. John Adams admitted that half of his clients left him. Josiah Quincy, Jr., received many angry and threatening letters, including one from Josiah Quincy, Sr., dated March 22, 1770:

> My Dear Son,
> I am under great affliction, at hearing the bitterest reproaches uttered against you, for having become an advocate for those criminals who are charged with the murder of their fellow citizens. Good God! Is it possible? I will not believe it . . .

The two lawyers defended their clients skillfully; most were acquitted, two were declared guilty of manslaughter and received light sentences. The withdrawal of the two regiments was attributed to the pressures of the mob—they were called "Sam Adams Regiments"—and the soldiers and their Tory sympathizers wrote many letters home describing the "disorderly mobs that ruled Boston." "You Simple Bostonians" was published as a broadside soon after with the introduction: "A new song much in vogue among the friends to arbitrary power, and the soldiery at Castle Island where it was composed, since the troops have evacuated the town of Boston."

The melody was well known to most Englishmen, having been for years the vehicle for ballads, comic songs, and political commentary.

# You Simple Bostonians

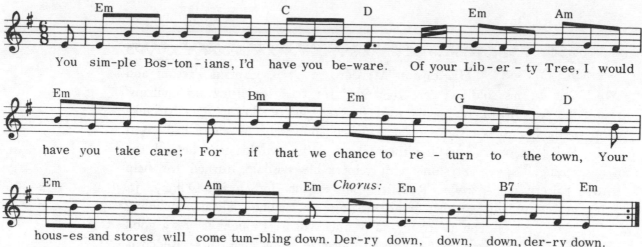

You sim-ple Bos-ton-ians, I'd have you be-ware. Of your Lib-er-ty Tree, I would

have you take care; For if that we chance to re-turn to the town, Your

hous-es and stores will come tum-bling down. *Chorus:* Der-ry down, down, down, der-ry down.

You simple Bostonians, I'd have you beware.
Of your Liberty Tree, I would have you take care;
For if that we chance to return to the town,
Your houses and stores will come tumbling down.
CHORUS: Derry down, down, down derry down.

If you'll not agree to obey England's laws,
I fear that King Hancock will soon get the yaws;
But he need not fear, for I swear we will,
For the want of a doctor give him a hard pill.
CHORUS:

A brave reinforcement, we soon think to get;
Then we will make you poor pumpkins to sweat;
Our drums they'll rattle, and then you will run,
To the devil himself, from the sight of a gun.
CHORUS:

Our fleet and our army, they soon will arrive,
And to a bleak island, you shall not us drive,
In every house, you shall have three or four,
And if that will not please you, you shall have half a score.
CHORUS:

New music arrangement and edited text © 1972 by Oscar Brand

THE WITHDRAWAL, following the Boston Massacre, of the two regiments from Boston seemed to herald an end to the power of the radicals to sway the mobs. As Benjamin Franklin wrote, "There seem to be among us violent spirits who are for an immediate rupture; but I trust that by our growing strength we advance fast to a situation in which our claims must be allowed."

But the peace was broken by many violent acts in the colonies. In June 1772, when the *Gaspee*, a Royal ship of war, ran aground while pursuing a smuggler, enraged Rhode Islanders clambered aboard, shot the captain, ordered the crew ashore, and burned the boat in the shallow water of Narragansett Bay. The Commission of Inquiry could find no one who had been in the vicinity of the hijacking, who knew anything of the incident, or who even understood the investigators' questions.

Emboldened by the success of their lawlessness, the rebellious group calling itself Sons of Liberty was able to recruit new members in all the colonies. They were helped by an announcement that Governor Thomas Hutchinson of Massachusetts and all Massachusetts judges would be paid by the Crown, and thus not be dependent on colonial support. Committees of Correspondence, which kept each colony informed of the events in other parts of the "country," began to develop as a conspiratorial network. What had been merely a news-gathering system was becoming a plan of organization for rebellion.

Nevertheless, there might have been no uprising, or concerted anger, had not Lord North, the First Lord of the Treasury, and the British Parliament passed the Tea Act. Their intention was really to save the British East India Company from bankruptcy. The King himself and many of his ministers owned stock in the Company, and its shares had plunged to almost half of what they had paid for them. North announced that the East India Company would be awarded the monopoly on sales of tea to the American colonies.

Furthermore, North's government would support the Company financially, thus enabling it to charge less for the tea than foreign companies. Benjamin Franklin was appalled, declaring: "The British Ministry have no idea that any people can act from any principle but that of interest, and they believe that three pence in a pound of tea, of which one does perhaps drink ten pounds in a year, is sufficient to overcome all the patriotism of an American." The colonists wanted no monopolies, nor the loss of their own tea businesses, especially where executed by Royal appointees.

*Throwing the tea overboard*

In almost every American port the tea ships were either turned back, or their cargo unloaded to rot in the warehouses. But Governor Hutchinson of Massachusetts had appointed his two sons as tea agents, and refused to allow the tea ships to return to England unless the duty was paid. The Patriots insisted that the unfortunate ship owner, Francis Rotch, send his ship back to England. The Governor refused to give permission, and the Customs House officials, even in the presence of twelve angry "Persons," couldn't grant him clearance.

Meanwhile, thousands of citizens had gathered at Faneuil Hall in response to a widely distributed broadside:

Friends, brethren and country men, that worst of all plagues, the detested tea, shipped for this port by the East India Company, is now arrived in this harbor. The hour of destruction or manly opposition to the machinations of tyranny stares you in the face. Every friend to his country, to himself and to posterity, is now called upon to meet at Faneuil Hall, at nine o'clock this day (at which time the bells will ring) to make united and successful resistance to this last, worst, and most destructive measure of administration.

When the committee reported that the ship *Dartmouth* was stalemated in the harbor, Samuel Adams arose and announced, "Then this meeting can do nothing more to save the country." As if it were a prearranged signal, (which it probably was), there appeared a band of about 200 "Indians" who proceeded to board the ships and throw 342 chests of tea into the harbor.

According to one eyewitness, "They say the actors were Indians from Narragansett. Whether they were or not, to a transient observer they appear'd as such, being cloath'd in Blankets with the heads muffled, and copper-color'd countenances, being each arm'd with a hatchet or axe, and pair pistols." The "transient observer" is one of the few persons who didn't know that the "Indians" were Rebels and Patriots organized by Hancock and Adams.

The following song was written years later to describe the event, and is chosen because it is accurate and happily comic.

*The Boston Tea Party*

# The Tea Party

I snum I am a Yan-kee man and I'll sing to you a dit-ty, And if you don't ap-prove of it, the more's 'twill be the pi-ty. That is, I mean, I might have been a pla-guey sight more fin-ished man, Had I been born in Bos-ton town, but I warn't so I'm a coun-try-man. Fol-de-ral-de-ra, fol-de-ral-de-ray, But I warn't so I'm a coun-try-man.

I snum I am a Yankee man and I'll sing to you
  a ditty,
And if you don't approve of it, the more's
  'twill be the pity,
That is, I mean, I might have been a plague
  sight more finished man,
Had I been born in Boston town, but I warn't
  so I'm a country man.
CHORUS:
  Folderal deray, folderal deray,
  But I warn't so I'm a countryman.

Now the other day the folks round here were
  mad about the taxes,
And so they went like Indians dressed to split
  the chests with axes,
It was the spring of seventy-three and we felt
  really gritty,
The Mayor he'd have lead the rout, but Boston
  warn't a city,
CHORUS:
  Folderal deray, folderal deray,
  But Boston warn't a city.

New music and edited text © 1972 by Oscar Brand

And so aboard the ships we went our vengeance
  to administer,
We didn't care one tarnal bit for any King or
  Minister,
We made a plaguey mess of tea in one of the
  world's big dishes,
I mean we steeped it in the sea and treated all
  the fishes,
CHORUS:
  Folderal deray, folderal deray,
  And treated all the fishes.

It was down in State Street we decided we'd
  not pay the duty,
For we didn't care to pay the toll of any tax or
  booty,
That is in State Street would have been, but
  'twas King Street they called it then,
And the tax on tea it was so strong the women
  wouldn't scald it then.
CHORUS:
  Folderal deray, folderal deray,
  The women wouldn't scald it then.

And then a fearful thing occurred, the which
  we'd always dreaded:
Our leaders were to England sent and instantly
  beheaded,
That is, I mean, they would have been, if ever
  they'd been taken,
But our leaders they were never cotched, that's
  how they saved their bacon.
CHORUS:
  Folderal deray, folderal deray,
  That's how they saved their bacon.

*The Boston Tea Party*

THE BOSTON Tea Party was marvelously organized. None of the "savages" had been recognized, there had been no violence or looting, and the message of angry resistance had been made clear to all. When a "certain Captain" tried to hide some of the tea in his waistcoat, he was "stripped of his acquisition and very roughly handled." In a short time, riders were ranging through the colonies with the news. Loyalists, often called "Tories" for the King's party in Parliament, began writing angry letters to England demanding an end to the vandals and upstarts.

The ministry for colonial administration under Lord North had already decided to take repressive measures against the Rebels. In fact, even while the news of the Tea Party was still at sea, the Privy Council was deciding to try Benjamin Franklin for comforting and abetting the enemies of the Crown. Franklin had been writing anonymous satires in English magazines, and the King's spies had discovered his secret. On January 29, 1774, he was trussed and bound and brought before the Council in an official room known as the Cockpit. It was a bad moment for the news of the Tea Party to arrive.

Franklin had not approved of the Tea Party, and had even offered to pay for the lost tea out of his own pocket. But he was not allowed to mention this. He was surrounded by courtiers whom he despised, and who hated him in return. He had once observed, "If America would save for three or four years the money she spends in Fashions and Fineries and Fopperies of this Country, she might buy the whole Parliament, Minister and all."

The Solicitor General, General Alexander Wedderburn, accused Franklin of organizing a conspiracy to create an "American Republic." He was dismissed from his sinecure as deputy postmaster general, was assigned spies who opened his mail and dogged his footsteps, and was deprived of the open companionship of his many British friends. Further, against his advice, the Ministry announced a series of "Coercive Acts" by which the Port of Boston was closed to commerce, a Massachusetts Military Government was set up under General Thomas Gage, and troops were sent in great numbers to watch for and put down all sedition.

In America, the Acts were retitled the "Intolerable Acts" and Boston became the focus of colonial sympathy. Shepherds brought sheep to Boston, goatherds led their flocks to the Commons, food and clothing came tumbling in from heretofore competitive colonies to help the Bostonians in their need. Tories were set upon and beaten, and it was dangerous to be discovered drinking tea—any tea, even sassafras-brewed. The following song was written by a young lady in 1774 of whom little is known except that she was described as "A native of Virginia, endowed with all the graces of a cultivated mind, pleasant external qualities, and a model of patriotism worthy the emulation of many more conspicuous."

# Begone, Pernicious Tea

Begone, per - ni - cious bane - ful __ tea, With __ all Pan -
do - ra's ills __ pos - sessed. Hy - son, no more be - guiled __ by __
thee, My no - ble sons shall __ be op - pressed. __

Begone, pernicious, baneful tea,
With all Pandora's ills possessed.
Hyson, no more beguiled by thee,
My noble sons shall be oppressed.

To Britain fly, where gold enslaves,
And venal men their birthright sell,
Tell North and his bribed clan of knaves,
Their bloody acts were made in hell.

For we oppose and will be free,
This great good cause we will defend,
Nor bribe, nor Gage, nor North's decree,
Shall make us at his feet to bend.

Our King we love, but North we hate,
Nor will to him submission own,
If death's our doom, we'll brave our fate,
But pay allegiance to the throne.

Then rouse, my sons! from slavery free
Your suffering homes; from God's high wrath;
Gird on your steel; give liberty,
To all who follow in our path.

New music and edited text © 1972 by Oscar Brand

HINDSIGHT TELLS us that there was an almost inexorable movement to Revolution in the colonies. The few radicals became a host as each repressive measure was announced. The merchants, who might have proved a conservative brake against immoderate action, found it to their interest to defy the monarchial authority. The colonial administration was often halfhearted in their execution of the laws—sometimes be-

[ 29 ]

cause of bribery, sometimes due to a lack of conviction. And the great number of laborers or clerks thought of "freedom" as a direct route to prosperity.

There were enough Tories to overwhelm the rebellion—with the help of the authorities—but, except for some strength in New York and Philadelphia and in the South, they never mounted a successful counterattack. Perhaps it was because they were supporting an idea whose time had passed.

For instance one of the most outspoken Tories, an Anglican parson named Jonathan Boucher, delivered a sermon on Civil Liberty in Maryland which was repeated and reprinted throughout the colonies:

"... True liberty is a liberty to do every thing that is right, and the being restrained from doing any thing that is wrong. ... The supreme magistrate, whether consisting of one or of many, and whether denominated an emperor, a king, an archon, a dictator, a consul, or a senate, is to be regarded and venerated as the vice-regent of God.

But few accepted Boucher's antiquated ideas. Even in England, the King had to use bribes and force to achieve his aims. The concept of a divinely endowed monarch hadn't survived the end of the seventeenth century and the middle class was too powerful to submit to arbitrary laws. It would have been wise had the Court been moderate with the rebellion.

But the Court was not wise. The late Winston Churchill listed at least four reasons for this lack of wisdom: first, there was the selfish doctrine that the colonies existed only for the benefit of the Mother Country; second, there was the desperate hunger for money to fill a bankrupt exchequer; third, there was jealousy of colonial competition in the sugar industry centering in the West Indies; and fourth, there was the counsel of Army advisers who despised the colonial troops and underrated the problem of subduing and conquering a sullen populace in a distant land.

Two of the "Coercion Acts" were very effective in uniting the colonies in opposition to British rule. One decreed that all judges were to be appointed by the Crown. Another provided that British troops could be quartered in every colony. The colonial assemblies called a congress in Philadelphia which demanded the rescinding of thirteen British Acts. The petition was rejected.

General Gage, Commander of British troops in the colonies, issued a stern proclamation which was satirized in ballad form with further inflammatory results.

# Gage's Proclamation

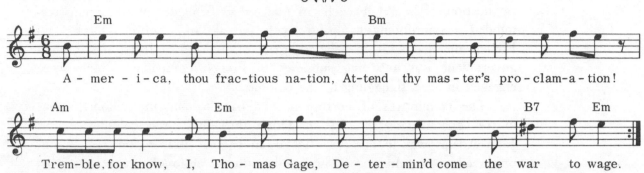

A—mer—i–ca, thou frac-tious na-tion, At-tend thy mas-ter's pro-clam-a-tion!

Trem-ble.for know, I, Tho—mas Gage, De—ter—min'd come the war to wage.

America, thou fractious nation,
Attend thy master's proclamation!
Tremble, for know, I, Thomas Gage,
Determin'd come the war to wage.

With the united powers sent forth,
Of Bute, of Mansfield, and of North,
To scourge your insolence, my choice,
While England mourns and Scots rejoice.

Bostonia first shall feel my power,
And gasping midst the dreadful shower,
Of ministerial rage, shall cry,
Oh, save me, Bute! I yield, and die.

Whistle, ye pipes, ye drones drone on,
Ye bellows blow! Virgina's won!
Your Gage has won Virginia's shore,
And Scotia's sons shall mourn no more.

Thy sons obedient, naught shall fear,
Thy wives and widows drop no tear,
Fear Bute, fear Mansfield, North, and me,
And be as blest as slaves can be.

New music and edited text © 1972 by Oscar Brand

BY 1774 disobedience to the Crown and rebellion against British law
had become an institution. Americans smuggled at least 5,000 chests
of tea from Holland alone, and it is believed that many of these chests
contained gunpowder. So many British firms were running arms to America
that in October 1774, the British Council forbade the export of arms to
America in a public order. Rather than lose such a profitable trade, British

firms began shipping contraband to the island of St. Eustatius in the Caribbean. It was well known that American merchants were loading their ships with this illegal cargo.

Furthermore, evidence has recently been unearthed, as a result of publication of secret French archives, that Benjamin Franklin masterminded a gunrunning campaign with the aid of English, Dutch, and French merchants. It is believed that, through his efforts, the French government was awarding subsidies to French companies which were engaged in arms smuggling to the colonies.

The committees of correspondence had become intercolonial committees guaranteeing a unity of action throughout the colonies. Later, John Adams was to observe, "What an engine! France imitated it and produced a revolution." These committees, although representing a minority of the colonists, were able to silence opposition, and frighten uncertain men into militance. "The threat of tyranny and the terror of slavery are artfully set before them; a measure need only be proposed to be resolved upon—a measure from which a little reflection would have made them react in horror," observed one royalist.

In May 1774, Maryland defied the committees, as had other colonies, and refused to protest the Boston Port Bill. But by December deputies appointed by "the freemen of the province of Maryland" unanimously resolved to resist the authority of Parliament. They even recommended that every man should provide himself with "a good firelock, with bayonet attached, powder and ball, and be in readiness to act in any emergency." This "Resolve" was forwarded to the new Continental Congress, which was a collection of the leading Committeemen from the colonies; it was to become the main organ of Sedition and Rebellion.

The Loyalists and the Tories were unorganized, but they had among their ranks many fine satirists and balladeers. One of them wrote this song, which seems at first to be a revolutionary ballad, but was published in Rivington's *Gazette*, a Loyalist paper, with the accompanying letter:

> You, no doubt, have seen the resolves of certain magnates, naming themselves a Provincial Congress! I will not say these worthies are under the influence of the moon, or are proper subjects for confinement, but one of their resolves is exactly calculated for the meridian of the inquisition, and the others smell furiously of Bedlam.

Calvert, mentioned in the song, was the original colonist of Maryland.

# The Maryland Resolves

On    Cal-vert's plains    new fac - tion reigns, Great Brit - ain    we    de - fy,    sir.    True
lib - er - ty    lies gagg'd    in    chains, Though free - dom    is    the    cry,    sir.    The
Con - gress and    their fac - tious tools,    most wan - ton - ly    op - press    us.    Hy-
poc - ri - sy    tri - um - phant rules    and sore - ly    does    dis - tress    us.

On Calvert's plains new faction reigns,
Great Britain we defy, sir.
True liberty lies gagg'd in chains,
Though freedom is the cry, sir.
The Congress and their factious tools,
Most wantonly oppress us,
Hyprocrisy triumphant rules,
And sorely does distress us.

The British bands with glory crown'd,
No longer shall withstand us.
Our martial deeds loud fame shall sound,
Since mad Lee now commands us.
Triumphant soon a blow he'll strike,
That all the world shall awe, sir,

And Gen'ral Gage, sir, Perseuslike,
Behind his wheels he'll draw, sir.

When Gallic hosts, ungrateful men,
Our race meant to extermine,
Pray, did committees save us then,
Or Hancock, or such vermin?
Then faction spurn, think of yourselves,
Your parent state, believe me,
From real griefs, from factious elves,
Will speedily relieve ye.

*General Gage*

New music and edited text © 1972 by Oscar Brand

[ 33 ]

BY 1774 General Gage was in Boston with 4,000 British troops. Fearful Loyalists began taking refuge in the city, writing resentful letters home expressing such hopes as "The Rebels would swing for it" and would "become turnspits in the kitchen of some English noble," eagerness to see "blood streaming from the hearts of the leaders," and a desire to one day "ride through American blood to the hubs of our chariot wheels."

One night in September 1774, Loyalists sent a letter to Boston's British headquarters, as follows: "The friends of your king and country and of America hope and expect it from you soldiers that the instant rebellion happens that you will put the above persons immediately to the sword, destroy their homes and plunder their effects." "The above persons" proscribed identified such radicals as "Samuel Adams, James Bowdoin, Dr. T. Young, Dr. B. Church, Cap. J. Bradford, Josiah Quincy, Major N. Barber, Wm. Molineaux, John Hancock, Wm. Cooper, Dr. Chaney, Dr. Cooper, Thos. Cushing, Jos. Greenleaf, and Wm. Denning."

Gage didn't really need the information, since one of the listed "radicals," one of the leading orators, pamphleteers, and hotheads of the rebellion, was on the British payroll. Paul Revere's Rebel-spy apparatus guessed that there was a leak somewhere, but no one suspected Dr. B. Church, who was, after all, a leading member of the Committee of Safety. Eventually he became the director of Medical Services for Washington's Army.

Gage was informed that the colonials were drilling 10,000 militiamen. He was also warned that the Massachusetts Assembly was meeting illegally in Concord, twenty miles from British headquarters in Boston. Moreover, Concord was the secret collection point for the arms and munitions smuggled in from the West Indies, England, and Holland. Here was Gage's chance to disarm the Rebels, capture their leaders, and spike the revolution until reinforcements could arrive.

April 18, 1775, 800 Redcoats set out secretly for Concord. But Paul Revere's spy organization was watching every gesture of the enemy. The munitions were moved in the night to Worcester, Massachusetts, while the leaders of the rebellion, John Hancock and Samuel Adams, were roused from sleep and escorted from Concord. The entire countryside was roused. At dawn the British silently and stealthily arrived in Lexington to discover 70 hostile militiamen waiting for them on the village green.

At this point, the reports are confused. The British and Loyalists claim that Major John Pitcairn of the Royal Marines, commanding the column, shouted, "Disperse, you Rebels, immediately!" There was the sound of a gunshot and the British responded automatically. One source claims that the leader of the militia called out, "Hold your fire, men, but if they mean to have a war, let it begin here." The *Virginia Gazette* reported, "They ordered them to disperse and immediately fired on them."

Whichever side began the action, all agreed on the following consequences, as reported in the *Gazette*:

They killed eight rebels on the spot and then marched to Concord. This alarmed the country so that it seemed as if colonists came down from the clouds. This news coming to town, General Gage sent out another thousand men, with a large train of artillery. In the meantime, those troops at Concord had set fire to the courthouse. There an engagement ensued, and the King's troops retreated very fast, until they were reinforced with the troops the General had sent, but they did not stand long before the whole body gave way; retreating, and our men keeping up at their heels, loading and firing, until they got to Charlestown.

*Battle scene on the Lexington Common*

# The Revolutionary Alphabet

A stands for A - mer - i - cans, who nev - er will be slaves.

B's for Bos - ton's bra - ve - ry that ev - er free - dom saves.

C is for the Con - gress, which, though loyal, will be free.

D stands for de - fense a - gainst all force and ty - ran - ny. Stand

firm - ly A to Z We swear for - ev - er to be free!

A stands for Americans, who never will be slaves,

B's for Boston's bravery that ever freedom saves,

C is for the Congress, which, though loyal, will be free,

D stands for defense against all force and tyranny.

CHORUS:

Stand firmly, A to Z,
We swear forever to be free!

E stands for the evils which a civil war must bring,

F stands for a dreadful fate for people and for King,

G's for George, may Heaven give him wisdom, health, and grace,

H is for the hypocrites who wear the double face.                CHORUS:

J's for justice which the traitors now in pow'r defy,

K's the King again, who should to such the axe apply,

L's for London where he sits, to Honor ever true,

M's for Mansfield, who, it seems, doth hold another view.                CHORUS:

New music and edited text © 1972 by Oscar Brand

N is North who to the House the evil mandate brings,
O's for oaths, which seemingly bind subjects not their kings,
P stands for the people who their freedom would defend,
Q stands for the question, when will England's troubles end? CHORUS:

R stands for the Rebels, not in Boston, but at home,
S stands for the Stuarts, sent by Whigs abroad to roam,
T stands for the Tories who may try to bring them back,
V stands for the villains who have well deserved the rack. CHORUS:

W must stand for Wilkes, who us from warrants saved,
Y for York the New, now half-corrupted, half-enslaved,
Z we give to Zero, which refers to Tory minions,
Who threaten us with fire and sword to bias our opinions. CHORUS:

*Ethan Allen*

NOW THAT the war had begun, Americans looked northward to Canada. The Quebec Act, which had been announced by Lord North's ministry in 1774, still rankled. In the first place, it extended the boundaries of Quebec beyond the Alleghenies and south to the Ohio though this land had been claimed by Americans for many years. Secondly, it guaranteed the Roman Catholics of Canada protection of their ancient rights and practices. To the Protestant colonists this smacked of "Popery" and intertwining of Church and State.

*The Ruins of Ticonderoga*

The Continental Congress was filled with men who dreamed that Canada might be an American colony, separated from England. This would prevent England from using the northern country as an invasion route. Athwart this route was Fort Ticonderoga, a decrepit "stronghold" commanding the upper Hudson Valley. One early morning, on May 10, 1775, Patriot troops commanded by Ethan Allen and Colonel Benedict Arnold surprised this "amazing Useless Mass of Earth," as it was described, captured the garrison, and went on to take Crown Point and St. John's.

Ethan Allen, born in Connecticut, was a farmer in the Hampshire Grants, later named "Vermont." Benedict Arnold was a Connecticut colonel leading troops levied by the Provincial Congress of Massachusetts. The two and their men, known as "Green Mountain Boys," had captured a British fort which lay within the confines of New York. The Second Continental Congress wrested with the knotty problem—to whom did the conquest belong? A number of the Congressmen even suggested that Ticonderoga be returned to the Crown.

The fort did have a battery of cannons that was necessary to the Rebel cause, but experts agreed these couldn't be moved from the Fort to any strategic location. The main value of the conquest was obvious. The British couldn't easily bring land forces down the Hudson Valley. And so the way was prepared for a major assault on Canada.

Yet, the congress of delegates meeting in Carpenters' Hall in Philadelphia were not certain they wanted to invest their futures in a fratricidal war. There was no colonial army, no navy, no treasury, no common traditions which might bind the disparate colonies together. They knew that the British troops were about to be reinforced with fresh regiments on their way from England. Perhaps there might yet be peace.

For the militiamen, who had already tasted victory in battle, there could be no peace until the last British soldier had been expelled. Arnold's troops, the Minutemen of Captain John Parker, the leaderless company of Captain Isaac Davis, who had died at the North Bridge, these men would never stop fighting. And Ethan Allen's "Green Mountain Boys" until their commander, later in the war, offered the British a separate peace, continually sought to repeat their Ticonderoga triumph, singing this buoyant song.

# The Green Mountaineer

Ho, all to the bor-ders, Ver-mon-ters come down, With your breeches of deer-skin, your
jack-ets of brown, With your red wool-en caps and your moc-ca-sins, come, To the
gath-er-ing sum-mons of trum-pet and drum. Come down with your ri-fle, let
grey wolf and fox howl on in the sha-dow of prim-i-tive rocks, Let
bear feed se-cure-ly from pig-pen and stall. Here's two-legg-ed game for your
pow-der and ball. Then cheer, cheer, the Green Moun-tain-eer. ____

Ho, all to the borders, Vermonters come down,
With your breeches of deerskin, your jackets
    of brown,
With your red woolen caps and your moc-
    casins, come,
To the gathering summons of trumpet and
    drum.

Come down with your rifle, let gray wolf and
    fox
Howl on in the shadow of primitive rocks,
Let bear feed securely from pigpen and stall,
Here's two-legged game for your powder and
    ball.
CHORUS:
    Then cheer, cheer, the Green Mountaineer.

New music and edited text © 1972 by Oscar Brand

[ 40 ]

On the south came the Dutchman, enveloped
    in grease,
And armed for the battle while canting of
    peace,
On our east came the British, the redcoated
    bard,
To hang up our leaders and eat up our lard,
Ho, all to the rescue, for Satan shall work,
No gain for the legions of Hampshire and York.
They claim our possession, the pitiful knaves,
The tribute we pay shall be prisons and graves.
CHORUS:

We owe no allegience, we bow to no throne,
Our ruler is law and the law is our own.
Our leaders themselves are our own fellow men,
Who can handle the sword, or the scythe, or
    the pen,
Hurrah for Vermont, for the land that we till,
Must have sons to defend her from valley and
    hill,
Our vow is recorded, our banner unfurled,
In the name of Vermont, we defy all the world.
CHORUS:

B RITISH GENERAL Thomas Gage decided to wait in Boston until reinforcements could arrive from England. However, on May 13, 1775, he received a letter from the informer, Dr. Benjamin Church, informing him that the Americans meant to occupy Bunker Hill, which towered over his headquarters from nearby Charlestown Peninsula. Gage had no reason to doubt the authority of the spy, since, with Hancock and Adams away at the Continental Congress, Dr. Church was, by default, leader of the Massachusetts rebels.

On May 25, the reinforcements arrived, commanded by general Clinton, Howe, and Burgoyne. In a council of war they decided to occupy Charlestown Peninsula on June 18. This information was immediately conveyed to the Patriot, Dr. Joseph Warren, by the Rebel spy, James Lovell. That James Lovell should be a Rebel spy was only fair since his father, John Lovell, was a spy for the British. Dr. Warren announced, "These fellows say we won't fight; by heavens, I hope I shall die up to my knees in blood." And the Massachusetts Committee of Safety decided to fortify Bunker Hill before the British could forestall them.

Ordinarily, Dr. Church would have informed Gage of this decision, but this time Dr. Church didn't know of the plan—he was on his way to Philadelphia with important dispatches for Hancock and Adams. That is why, on the morning of June 17, the British were astounded to discover more than a thousand Rebels behind six-foot redoubts on Breed's Hill. It is true that the orders had been to fortify Bunker Hill, but the Patriot leaders, General Israel Putnam and Colonel William Prescott, during the night, led their men to the wrong hill.

With all his artillery and ship's cannon, Gage could have easily blown the Rebels off the mountain or isolated them by capturing the narrow neck of the Peninsula. But he wanted to show the Rebels what real soldiering was, and he decided on a frontal assault. Twenty-eight barges were rowed across the water, fifty men to a barge, twelve field pieces in the first two barges. As soon as these were unloaded, the barges returned for more men, until there were almost 3,000 of Britain's finest ready for the attack. Meanwhile the fleet pounded the Rebel positions, and cannons from the mainland devastated the Rebel ranks.

General Putnam suddenly noticed Dr. Warren among the front line troops. Warren, President of the Provincial Congress, had recently been appointed Major General. Putnam asked for orders, but Warren pointed out that his official appointment papers had not come through and he was to be considered merely as a volunteer. The sound of the skirling British war pipes was heard. British commander, General Howe was extorting his men, "You must drive these farmers from the hill or it will be impossible for us to remain in Boston. But I shall not desire any of you to advance a single step beyond where I am at the head of your line."

The Redcoats climbed the hill in perfect battle array. They were less than fifty yards from the breastworks when "the farmers" rose up and loosed a terrible volley. The smoke was blinding, and men were shrieking and dying on all sides. Three times the British climbed the Hill. The last time the Rebels were firing bent nails and scraps of metal snatched off the ground, throwing rocks, and cursing the lack of ammunition.

It was bayonet against clubbed rifles, fearful men wrestling with an enemy they could hardly see. Ammunition ran out. With his last ball, a black man named Salem Prince shot Major John Pitcairn—the officer who had commanded the British at Lexington. As the Rebels finally retreated from Breed's Hill another ball took the life of Dr. Joseph Warren—who had written the following song.

# Free Amerikay

Torn from a world of ty-rants, be-neath this west-ern sky, We formed a new do-min-ion, a land of lib-er-tie. The world shall own we're mas-ters here, then has-ten on the day, Huz-za, huz-za, huz-za, huz-za for free A-mer-i-cay.

Torn from a world of tyrants, beneath this western sky,
We formed a new dominion, a land of liberty.
The world shall own we're masters here, then hasten on the day,
Huzza, huzza, huzza, huzza, for free Amerikay.

Lift up your hands, ye heroes, and swear with proud disdain,
The wretch that would ensnare you shall lay his snares in vain,
Should Europe empty all her force we'll meet her in array,
And fight and shout, and fight and shout for free Amerikay.

God bless this maiden climate and through its vast domain,
May hosts of heroes cluster who scorn to wear a chain.
Then guard your rights, Americans, nor stoop to lawless sway,
Oppose, oppose, oppose, oppose for North Amerikay.

Some future day shall crown us the masters of the main,
Our fleets shall speak in thunder to England, France, and Spain.
And nations o'er the ocean spread shall tremble and obey,
The sons, the sons, the sons, the sons of free Amerikay.

New music arrangement and edited text © 1972 by Oscar Brand

[ 43 ]

*Prescott at the defense of Breed's Hill*

THE BATTLE for Breed's Hill in 1775, which is often called "Bunker Hill," was a turning point in many ways. It was not a haphazard, frightened meeting, but a carefully chosen field of combat. It is of little importance today that General Putnam chose to fortify Breed's Hill instead of the easier-to-defend heights of Bunker's Hill. That any choice was made, and that a battle was joined between two disciplined forces, indicated a declaration of war. When Gage, after taking the heights, offered free pardon to all Rebels who would lay down their arms, it was a useless gesture. The decision to take up arms was made before the battle and was maintained in full view of overpowering British force.

In one other way the Battle figured importantly in the conduct of the Revolution. Four of England's finest officers led the attack—General Gage, the supreme commander, General William Howe, General Henry Clinton, and General John Burgoyne. Later in the war, as each took command of his own army, the memory of Bunker Hill influenced every decision. In their memoirs, in their battle orders, in their letters to friends at home, the terrible carnage of Bunker Hill seemed to infuse their thoughts of the war with an unmilitary melancholy. Historians have pointed out that it was only later in the years of the Revolution that a major British commander appeared on the scene who was not obsessed by the memory of Bunker Hill—Lord Charles Cornwallis.

Directly after the battle, each side claimed a victory. The Rebels pointed out that of the 2,000 left dead or wounded on the slope, almost 1,500 of them were British regulars. Furthermore, there was no longer any question that loosely organized militiamen would stand before the well-drilled charge of a veteran army. When Washington heard the news, he exclaimed, "The liberties of the country are safe."

Nevertheless, the Rebels had retreated and the British had recovered the Hill. Gage sent off self-congratulatory reports to London, and announced an extra ration of rum for his victorious soldiers. Tories rejoiced that the fanatics had finally been punished for their treason. But one poet posted the following, unsigned, on a large handbill:

Warlike casuists can't discuss if we beat them, or they beat us,
We swear we beat, they swear we lie, we'll tell you more on't bye and
    bye.

And the following song, whose author is also anonymous, describes the battle as less than a glorious victory for either side.

# Bunker Hill

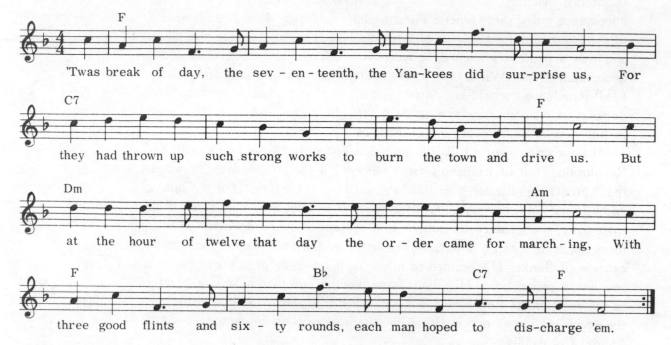

'Twas break of day, the sev-en-teenth, the Yan-kees did sur-prise us, For
they had thrown up such strong works to burn the town and drive us. But
at the hour of twelve that day the or-der came for march-ing, With
three good flints and six-ty rounds, each man hoped to dis-charge 'em.

'Twas break of day, the seventeenth, the Yankees did surprise us,
For they had thrown up such strong works to
burn the town and drive us.
But at the hour of twelve that day the order
came for marching,
With three good flints and sixty rounds, each
man hoped to discharge 'em.

We marched down to the Long Wharf where
the boats were ready waiting,
With expedition we embarked, our ships kept
cannonading,
And when our boats were all filled up we
rowed in line of battle,
Where showers of ball like hail did fly, and
cannon loud did rattle.

Brave William Howe, on our right wing cried,
"Boys, fight on like thunder,
You soon will see the Rebels flee with great
amaze and wonder,"

They turned their fire on our left, which Pigot
he commanded,
But we returned it back again, 'tis wonder they
could stand it.

And when their works were got into they
would not take to flight, sir,
But came at us stocks and stores and showed
us they could fight, sir,
We brought up our artillery and finally they
run, sir,
But while their ammunition held, they gave us
Yankee fun, sir.

Such stalwart Whigs I never saw, to hang them
all I'd rather,
Their cursed skill with musket balls sure caused
us such a bother,
To yield the height at Bunker Hill they made
us pay full dearly,
And Howe will not forget the day they used
us so severely.

New music and edited text © 1972 by Oscar Brand

*The Battle of Bunker Hill*

THE DAY before the Battle of Bunker Hill in 1775 an event occurred which was probably even more important than the inspiring heroism of the Rebel army. The dispatches that Benjamin Church carried to the Second Continental Congress requested that the New England army be designated as an "American Army," and that a central government be set up to administer the general affairs of the colonies. The debate began and the delegates argued over the man who might command a colonial army. General Artemas Ward was suggested since he was already in charge of the Yankees blockading the British in Boston. John Hancock wanted the command for himself. After all, he *was* the president.

But John Adams, afraid that the war might look like a New England monopoly, stated:

> I had no hesitation to declare that I had but one gentleman in my mind for that important command, and that was a gentleman from Virginia who was among us and very well known to all of us, a gentleman whose skill and experience as an officer, whose independent fortune, great talents, and excellent universal character, would command the approbation of all Americans, and unite the cordial exertions of all the Colonies better than any other person in the Union. . . . Mr. Hancock—while I was speaking on the state of the Colonies, the army at Cambridge, and the enemy—heard me with visible pleasure; but when I came to describe Washington for the commander, I never remarked a more sudden and striking change of countenance. Mortification and resentment were expressed as forcibly as his face could exhibit them.

Samuel Adams seconded the motion, there was a spirited debate, but on June 16, 1775, John Hancock announced the unanimous appointment of Colonel George Washington of Virginia to command the American Army. Immediately the commander-in-chief set out for Cambridge to take over from General Artemas Ward. He arrived in a rainstorm, July 2, 1775, to discover that General Ward had cancelled the expected reception because of the weather, and that no one appeared enthusiastic over his appointment.

The Tories in Boston were well-informed concerning the new developments and viewed them with mixed feelings. The British had ignored their warnings and advice, and more than one echoed the resentment toward George's government expressed in the following letter: "I want those conceited islanders to learn by some knock-down, irrefragable argument that our continent can furnish brave soldiers and judicious expert commanders." And because the Tories considered Washington an "expert commander," they were gentle to him even in their most bitter satires.

[ 48 ]

# The Trip to Cambridge

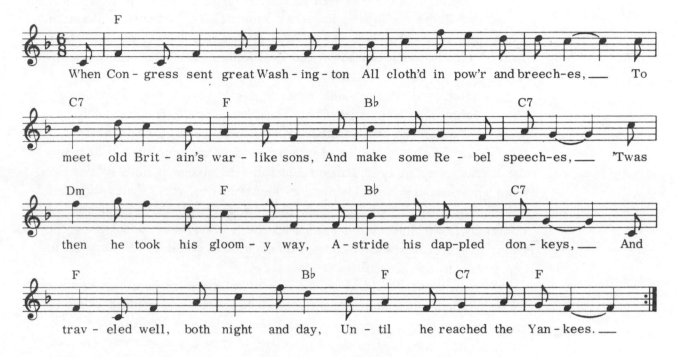

*Election Scene1*
When Congress sent great Washington
All clothed in pow'r and breeches,
To meet old Britain's warlike sons,
And make some Rebel speeches,
'Twas then he took his gloomy way,
Astride his dappled donkeys,
And traveled well, both night and day,
Until he reached the Yankees.

*Commission Scene2*
Away from camp, not three miles off,
From Lily he dismounted,
His sergeant brushed his sunburned wig,
While he his money counted.
Old Mother Hancock with a pan,
All sputtering with butter,
Unto the lovely Georgious ran,
And added to the splutter.

Full many a child went down to camp,
All dressed in homespun Kersey,
To see the greatest Rebel scamp,
That ever crossed o'er Jersey.
Upon a stump he placed himself,
Great Washington did he,
And standing on his timber shelf,
Proclaimed Great Liberty.

*Scene3*

New music and edited text © 1972 by Oscar Brand

ON JULY 10, Washington, having examined the military lines about Boston, wrote to the Continental Congress to acquaint them with a few of his problems: "We are as well secured as could be expected in so short a time and under the disadvantages we labor. These consist in a Want of Tools, and a sufficient Number of Men to man the Works in Case of an attack." He also noted a want of money, clothing, engineers, and ammunition.

Congress was at the same time receiving pleas from Ticonderoga, Crown Point, and New York City. The New York Committee of Safety wrote, "We have no arms, we have no powder, we have no blankets. For God's sake, send us money, send us arms, send us ammunition." Where was the ammunition? In 1774, Patriots had captured 10,000 pounds of powder from an arsenal in New Hampshire. In May 1775, the Liberty Boys of Savannah, Georgia, took about six tons off a British ship. Shipments of munitions from Holland and France had been very heavy, and yet by the end of August, there wasn't enough ammunition available to Washington to enable him to use his artillery.

It is believed that local committees of safety were hoarding supplies for self-protection, and that many merchants were withholding stores of ammunition until the prices rose. Under the direction of Benjamin Franklin, the colonies were asked to ship supplies of brimstone and saltpeter to Congress, so that ammunition could be manufactured.

Franklin was everywhere, intriguing with French diplomats, writing letters to sympathetic officials in England, engineering the theft of gunpowder from the Royal arsenal in Bermuda. He served on overworked committees which were treating with the Indians and the Quakers; he was involved with the currency, and the organizing of a "United Colonies of North America," including Ireland, Canada, Nova Scotia, the West Indies, and the Floridas.

Franklin realized that, despite Concord, Lexington, and Breed's Hill, most of his fellow delegates to the Continental Congress did not really want independence. They were approving an "Olive Branch" petition to George III, pleading with the sovereign to protect them against the evil Parliament. Franklin knew what the answer would be, but he could not convince the Congress that the petition was useless.

Meanwhile, the rebellious colonials were creating new songs calling for "a capital chop" (Independence), and "a dance on the Liberty tree" (hanging for the Loyalists). The writer of the song, however, carefully avoided criticizing supporters of the American colonies in Parliament. William Pitt, the Earl of Chatham, and others were all supporters of the American cause.

# What a Court

(SEE "*You Simple Bostonians*" FOR THE MUSIC)

What a court hath old England of folly and sin,
Spite of Chatham and Camden, Barre, Burke,
  Wilkes, and Glynn!
Not content with the game act, they tax fish
  and sea,
And America drench with hot water and tea.
CHORUS:
  Derry down, down, down derry down.

But if the wise council of England doth think,
They may be enslaved by the power of drink,
They're right to enforce it; but then, do you
  see?
The colonies, too, may refuse and be free.
                         CHORUS:

There's no knowing where this oppression will
  stop;
Some say—there's no cure but a capital chop;
And that I believe's each American's wish,
Since you've drench'd them with tea, and
  depriv'd them of fish.       CHORUS:

Three generals these mandates have borne
  'cross the sea,
To deprive 'em of fish and to make 'em drink
  tea;
In turn, sure, these freemen will boldly agree;
To give 'em a dance upon Liberty Tree.
                         CHORUS:

Then *Freedom's* the word, both at home and
  abroad,
And damn every scabbard that hides a good
  sword!
Our forefathers gave us this freedom in hand,
And we'll die in defense of the rights of the
  land.                    CHORUS:

New music arrangement and edited text © 1972 by Oscar Brand

WHILE THE Continental Congress waited, following their Olive Branch petition, hoping for a Royal word that would mean peace, a notice was being posted throughout English towns:

By the King, a proclamation for suppressing rebellion and sedition. Whereas many of Our Subjects in divers Parts of Our Colonies and Plantations in North America, misled by dangerous and ill-designing Men, and forgetting the Allegiance which they owe to the Power that has protected and sustained them, after various disorderly Acts committed in Disturbance of the Publick Peace, to the Obstruction of lawful Commerce, and to the Oppression of Our loyal Subjects carrying on the same, have at length proceeded to an open and avowed Rebellion by arraying themselves in hostile Manner to withstand the Execution of the Law, and traitorously preparing, ordering, and levying War against Us. And whereas there is reason to apprehend that such Rebellion hath been much promoted and encouraged by the traitorous Correspondence, Counsels and Comfort of divers wicked and desperate Persons within this Realm . . .

It was August 23, 1775, and the King had decided that war was the only answer to the assault on the authority of his ministers.

In Boston, Gage and his 10,000 waited for the colonial Army to fall apart. Washington held his men together, although he dreaded the end of the year when most of the enlistments were bound to expire. Would the King relent before then? No one yet knew of the August 23rd proclamation in England. And so, on August 25, Jefferson was writing that he would rather be in dependence on Great Britain, properly limited, than on any nation on earth . . . and John Adams was writing home that reconcilation was still possible.

During this period of stalemate, sometimes called "The Siege of Boston," spies walked freely through British headquarters in Boston, and through American headquarters in Cambridge. One British spy enjoyed the confidence of General Israel Putnam, and often dined with the captain of Washington's guard. Two French spies joined the Rebels as volunteers, and gathered as much information as possible before sailing to London to report to the French Ambassador.

And Gage refused to move against the dwindling Rebel forces. Boston was full now of Tory refugees petitioning to be mustered into the British Army. There were over 6,500 able-bodied Tories eager to fight. Gage refused their help. Provisions in Boston were soon consumed. Winter was coming on and there was little fuel available but Gage still refused to move. Meanwhile the Rebels sang defiantly of their bravery and courage, and tauntingly reminded the Redcoats of their pitiful showing at Lexington and Concord.

# To the Troops in Boston

By my faith but I think you're all mak-ers of bulls, With your
brains in your breech-es, your feet in your skulls, Get home with your
mus-kets and put up your swords, And look in your book for the
mean-ing of words. You see now, my hon-ies, how much you're mis-
ta-ken, For Con-cord by dis-cord can nev-er be ta-ken.

By my faith, but I think you're all makers of
  bulls,
With your brains in your breeches, your feet
  in your skulls,
Get home with your muskets and put up your
  swords,
And look in your book for the meaning of
  words,
You see now, my honies, how much you're
  mistaken,
For Concord by discord can never be taken.

How brave you set out with your muskets so
  bright,
And thought to bedazzle the folks with the
  sight,
But when you got there how they powdered
  your pums,

And all the way home how they peppered your
  bums,
And is it not, honies, a comical crack,
To be proud in the face and be shot in the back.

And what have you got now with all your
  designing,
But a town without victuals to sit down and
  dine in,
And to look at the ground like a parcel of
  noodles,
And to sing, "How the Redcoats have beaten
  the Doodles,"
I'm sure, if you're wise, you'll make peace for
  a dinner,
For fighting and fasting will soon make you
  thinner.

New music and edited text © 1972 by Oscar Brand

THE MEMBERS of the Second Continental Congress believed that the people of Canada would join the rebellion if only some incident could spark their enthusiasm for the Cause. Then there came disturbing news from a Yale-graduated backwoodsman named John Brown who was friendly with the border tribes and French voyageurs. He had learned that General Sir Guy Carleton, British Commander of Canada, was building a fleet of small boats. The conclusion was inescapable. The British were mounting an invasion. The spark would have to be hurried.

General Philip Schuyler was in charge of the northern New York troops, but he was away when the news of the possible British attack arrived, and so his second-in-command, General Richard Montgomery, one-time member of Parliament, decided to destroy the British flotilla, and possibly conquer Canada at the same time. Despite sickness, almost impassable swamps and forests, scarcity of supplies, and drenching rains, Montgomery captured Fort St. John's, taking prisoner Major John André, and pressed on to the St. Lawrence River, where he occupied Montreal.

When the news reached Cambridge, Washington was thrilled with the possibility of a quick conquest. He decided to order one of his best officers, Colonel Benedict Arnold, to take a diversionary force up through Maine to Quebec. One thousand volunteers left Cambridge on September 13. No one but Benedict Arnold could have held the little striking force together through the terrible march. Provisions were lost when the little boats were capsized in the rapids, the weather was impossible, the snow impassable. When one division turned back in despair, the others exulted that there'd be fewer mouths to feed.

On December 2, Arnold joined forces with Montgomery near Quebec. He had only 650 men left, while Montgomery had no more than 400. Although they were undermanned, they had to move quickly, for at the end of December, the terms of enlistment would run out, and most of the remaining soldiers would certainly turn back and make for their homes.

On December 30 they attacked. Montgomery was killed, Arnold was wounded, and the British took as prisoners 300 men including Captain Daniel Morgan and Lieutenant Colonel Christopher Greene, General Nathanael Greene's cousin. The few remaining troops retreated homeward, carrying Arnold with them. Afterward there appeared in print "A New Song, to the Tune 'Yankee Doodle'" with the comment, ". . . written at Quebec soon after the late siege thereof."

# Arnold Is As Brave a Man

Ar - nold is as brave a man as ev - er dealt in hor - ses, And
now com - mands a nu - m'rous clan of New Eng - land jack - ass - es.

*Chorus:*

Yan - kee Doo - dle, keep it up, Yan - kee Doo - dle Dan - dy,

Mind the mu - sic and the step and with the girls be han - dy.

Arnold is as brave a man as ever dealt in horses,
And now commands a num'rous clan of New
  England jackasses,
CHORUS:
  Yankee Doodle, keep it up, Yankee Doodle
    dandy,
  Mind the music and the step and with the
    girls be handy.

With sword and spear he vows and swears that
  Quebec shall be taken,
But if he'd be advised by me, he'd fly to save
  his bacon.           CHORUS:

But t'other day he did assay to do some
  execution,
But he thought fit to run away for want of
  resolution.           CHORUS:

The next come in was Colonel Green, a black-
  smith by his trade, Sir,
As great a black as e'er was seen, tho' he's a
  Colonel made, Sir.        CHORUS:

The Congress, who're a noted set of very
  honest fellows,
On Yankee business being met told Green to
  sell his bellows.         CHORUS:

They gave him a commission straight and bid
  him not abuse it,
Told him his rusty sword to whet and sent him
  here to use it.          CHORUS:

'Tis thus, my friends, we are beset by all those
  damn'd invaders,
No greater villains ever met than are those
  Yankee traitors.         CHORUS:

*Washington before he was appointed to command the Army*

BY THE end of 1775 the Rebels feared that Washington's small army besieging the British in Boston would be miniscule—their eight-month terms of duty at an end. In September of 1775 the Rebels received another blow. General Putnam came riding up to Washington's headquarters with a pretty young lady behind him, whose story frightened the high command into a near panic. She was carrying a coded letter from a high colonial official to British headquarters. Although Washington warned her that "nothing but a full confession could save her from the halter . . . she was proof against every threat and persuasion to discover the Author."

At last she admitted that the letter was from Dr. Benjamin Church, and the letter, deciphered, was a systematic listing of American troop strength, rations, ammunitions, artillery, and war plans. It was hard to believe that Church was a spy. He was a Harvard graduate! How many others were traitors? No one could be immune from suspicion now. All agreed that an example must be made of Church, but unfortunately, the new regulations set up by the Congress hadn't envisioned such treachery. It was decided to jail Church illegally until the end of the rebellion. When he was exiled later in the war, he set off for the West Indies in a small schooner that was never heard from again.

The colonial cause was in a bad way. Had Gage known it, he could have walked his troops out of Boston with little trouble—Washington was out of ammunition, and depending on short-term militia to give his army the semblance of a fighting force. But a fortuitous circumstance saved the Cause. This circumstance was embodied in the person of Thomas Paine, radical Englishman who was only lately arrived in America. With a letter of recommendation from Benjamin Franklin, he was appointed editor of *The Pennsylvania Magazine*. He hated King George and his ministers, never forgetting the ignominy of being dismissed from his job as a customs officer for trying to organize a strike.

He reminded his readers that there had been a real "Liberty Tree" in Boston, that the British had chopped it into firewood, and that it existed now only in the hearts of his adopted countrymen. In January 1776, he proceeded to write a pamphlet that sold a half-million copies, and sounded through the colonies like a revolutionary battle call. It began, "In the following pages I offer nothing more than simple facts, plain arguments, and common sense." The argument, called *Common Sense*, declared:

> The sun never shined on a cause of greater worth. 'Tis not the affair of a city, a country, a province, or a kingdom; but of a continent—of at least one-eighth part of the habitable globe. 'Tis not the concern of a day, a year, or an age; posterity are virtually involved in the contest, and will be more or less affected even to the end of time by the proceedings now. Now is the seed time of continental union, faith, and honor.

Paine called for an end to self-delusion, a recognition of the King's repressive role, and a new order in the New World. He spoke, argued, harangued, fought, and wrote poems and pamphlets to support his beliefs. He even composed ballads on the subject. The following, written in 1775, is one of his best-known.

# Liberty Tree

In a chariot of light from the regions of day,
The Goddess of Liberty came.
Ten thousand celestials directed the way,
And hither conducted the dame.
A fair budding branch from the gardens above,
Where millions with millions agree,
She brought in her hand as a pledge of her love,
And the plant she named "Liberty Tree."

Beneath this fair tree, like the patriarchs of old,
Their bread in contentment they ate.
Unvex'd with the troubles of silver and gold,
The cares of the grand and the great,
With timber and tar they Old England
    supply'd,
And supported her pow'r on the sea;
Her battles they fought, without getting a
    groat,
For the honor of Liberty Tree.

New music and edited text © 1972 by Oscar Brand

But hear, o ye swains, 'tis a tale most profane,
How all the tyrannical pow'rs,
Kings, Commons and Lords, are uniting amain,
To cut down this guardian of ours.
From the east to the west blow the trumpet to
   arms,
Thro' the land let the sound of it flee,
Let the far and the near, all unite with a cheer,
In defense of our Liberty Tree.

*The Pine Tree Flag*

NO ONE has been able to prove the origin of one of the most popular marching songs of the Revolution. One tale attributes it to a legendary British Army Surgeon named Richard Shuckburgh, who was writing a satire about colonial militiamen in the French and Indian War. The lyrics certainly make fun of the Yankee Doodles for trying to maintain a military bearing despite an inborn gracelessness.

From the British point of view, the song proved of dubious value. First the Rebels expropriated it as a marching tune. Then it served to lull the British High Command into a feeling of security in the face of such bumpkins as those described in the song. It was well-known that Washington and many of his officers learned their trade in the militia. One of these militia Doodles was young Henry Knox.

Knox was a young Irish immigrant who had to go to work at the age of nine to help support his family. Working as a clerk in a bookselling company, he read book after book on military tactics, and was one of the few commanders who had more than a small practical knowledge of the art of war.

Knox fell in love with the daughter of one of New England's most prominent Tories. Thomas Flucker was an American aristocrat and his daughter, Lucy, had been raised as if she were a young lady of the British court. The Fluckers were outraged when their daughter announced that she wanted to marry Knox. Not only was he low-born, but he was also reputed to be in sympathy with the radicals. Knox managed to hide his advocacy of the Rebel cause until Lucy's family accepted the inevitable. They were married in June 1774, and, after refusing his father-in-law's offer of a commission in the British Army, Knox fled with Lucy to Washington's headquarters in Cambridge.

Knox designed new fortifications for Washington and was appointed commander of artillery. There wasn't much artillery to command, so the young officer suggested he ride north to Ticonderoga and bring back the cannons Ethan Allan and Benedict Arnold had liberated. Washington accepted the young man's eager offer, with little hope of seeing a successful effort. With the guns he could take Boston, but Ticonderoga was in another world with snow-covered mountain ranges lying between. Knox organized a small army of teamsters, hired sleds and oxen, and provisioned the enterprise for the hard winter ahead. That he brought back 59 cannons is one of the most remarkable achievements of the Revolution.

General Howe was now in full command of the British forces. He should have garrisoned Dorchester Heights, which looked down upon British Headquarters in Boston. But, like his predecessors, he had little respect for the "Yankee Doodles" arrayed against him. On the morning of March 5, 1776, he was awakened by a wide-eyed aide. Hurrying to the window, he discovered that Dorchester Heights, bare at sundown, was crowded with Rebel soldiers behind well-constructed fortifications, armed with a line of deadly-looking heavy artillery, courtesy of Henry Knox.

Howe decided that the honor of the British military required an attack on the Heights—which would probably have resulted in a bloody defeat. Fortunately, a terrible storm blew his transports up the bay, and he decided that Fate meant him to evacuate the city. And so, the British Army in Boston and many of the leading Tory families, including the Fluckers, set sail for Halifax, Nova Scotia. They were not singing as they sailed.

# Yankee Doodle Doodle Doo

(SEE "*Arnold Is As Brave a Man*" FOR THE MUSIC)

Father and I went down to camp along with
  Captain Goodin,
And there we saw the men and boys as thick
  as hasty puddin',
CHORUS:
    Yankee Doodle doodle doo, Yankee Doodle
     dandy,
    Mind the music and the step and with the
     girls be handy.

And there we saw a swamping gun, big as a
  log of maple,
Upon a little deuced cart, a load for father's
  cattle.           CHORUS:

And every time they fired it off, it took a horn
  of powder,
It made a noise like Father's gun, except a
  nation louder.       CHORUS:

And there we saw a thousand men as rich as
  Squire David,
And what they wasted every day I wish it
  could be savéd.      CHORUS:

And there was Captain Washington upon a
  strapping stallion,
A-giving orders to his men, there must've been
  a million.        CHORUS:

And then they marched and countermarched
  and made so great a bother,
I hooked it home and never stopped, until I saw
  my mother.       CHORUS:

Yankee Doodle is the tune Americans delight
  on,
It's pretty good for marching and it's just the
  thing to fight on.    CHORUS:

THE COLONIAL troops did not march triumphantly into Boston, with Washington at the head of the conquering army. The British fleet seemed to be watching offshore and there were British sentries on guard in the town. A few scouts probed the British defenses and discovered the "sentries" were dummies in Redcoats. The army followed soon after, and Washington rode in quietly and grimly prepared for whatever treachery the British might have waiting for him. As he observed, "The enemy have the best knack at puzzling people I ever met with in my life."

Though Howe's fleet finally took sail, he left behind a web of fantastic intrigue which included plans for a Tory uprising, sabotage of American ammunition dumps, and the kidnapping or poisoning of Lieutenant General Washington at his headquarters. These plans were flouted when a convicted counterfeiter revealed to the Congress confidences he had learned from a Tory who was a fellow prisoner.

Another conspiracy, one of the most impressive, was embodied in a plan to cut off the southern colonies from the headquarters in the north. Lord Dunmore, Royal Governor of Virgina, was gathering Loyalist forces who would join with a back-country regiment to be called "The Queen's Royal Rangers" in Detroit. These would fortify Alexandria, Virginia, and split the colonies. However, Dunmore lost the sympathy of most of the planters when he included in his orders a promise to free all slaves and indentured servants who would join his troops.

In South Carolina, Lord William Campbell, Royal Governor of the colony, had encouraged the commissioner for the southern Indians to turn the Catawba and Cherokee nations against the Rebels. And the British Government in England was also taking measures to meet the emergency. The *Freeman's Journal*, a Rebel publication, reported that the British government had

> . . . sent over to Germany to engage troops for American service, and succeeded in raising a legion of Jagers, people brought up in the use of the rifle-barrel guns, in boar hunting. They are amazingly expert, and the ministry plume themselves much in the thought of their being a complete match for the American riflemen.

This was a major blow to Washington's hopes. The colonial rifles had provided greater accuracy and distance. The British troops had used smooth-bore muskets, and had been outgunned consistently. Soon the Redcoats would be joined by German mercenaries who would wipe out the Rebel advantage.

One thing even the British admitted—the colonials could throw up fortifications with blinding speed. Even when the Tory press in Halifax printed anti-Rebel songs, one could detect a grudging respect for the "Burrowing Yankees" and their overnight investiture of Dorchester Heights.

# The Burrowing Yankees

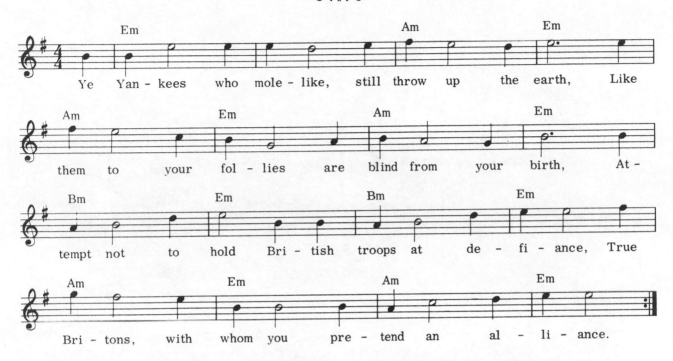

Ye Yan-kees who mole-like, still throw up the earth, Like them to your fol-lies are blind from your birth, At-tempt not to hold Bri-tish troops at de-fi-ance, True Bri-tons, with whom you pre-tend an al-li-ance.

Ye Yankees who, mole-like, still throw up the earth,
Like them to your follies are blind from your birth,
Attempt not to hold British troops at defiance,
True Britons, with whom you pretend an alliance.

Mistake not, such blood ne'er ran in your veins,
'Tis no more than dregs, or the lees, or the drains,
Ye affect to talk big of your hourly attacks,
Come on! and I'll warrant, we'll soon see your backs.

Such threats of bravados serve only to warm,
The true British heart you can never alarm,
The lion once rous'd will command such a terror,
And show you, poor fools, your presumption and error.

The time will soon come when your whole Rebel race,
Will be drove from the land, nor will dare show your face,
Here's a health to great GEORGE, may he fully determine,
To root out of the earth all such burrowing vermin.

New music and edited text © 1972 by Oscar Brand

*General Clinton's expedition against Charleston*

THOUGH THE Rebel leaders didn't know it, they had good reason to be grateful to British Intelligence. Spies and Tories were continually going to British headquarters announcing that in *their* home areas the people were waiting for a signal to rise to destroy the Revolution. With these reports in hand, British Intelligence decided that its next campaign should give southern Loyalists the leadership they needed to overcome the Rebels.

Virginia was already a lost cause to the British because Royal Governor Dunmore's men had been whipped by the Rebel militia in 1775. But North Carolina's Governor Josiah Martin equipped 1,500 American Tory highlanders for a march to the sea where the British Navy would be waiting. Why these Scotsmen, who considered themselves fugitives from British oppression, should fight for George III, is a puzzle that still confounds historians. But fight they did, in kilts and bonnets, waving claymores to the wild, thrilling wail of the war pipes. They arrived at Moore's Creek on February 27, 1776, and discovered an entrenched force of 1,000 Rebels. Bravely they marched on and were cut down by a deadly hail of rifle bullets. A total of 850 were captured, a dispirited army in bloody plaids.

Many other Tories were willing to prove their loyalty to the Crown by fighting the Rebellion. New York alone furnished 15,000 men to the British forces and over 8,000 Loyalist militia. But a few of the colonies, such as South Carolina, had not shown any great desire to be involved in a bloody war. Had British Intelligence realized this, they might have left Charleston alone and concentrated on the relatively weak and vulnerable Rebel army in the North.

Nevertheless, General Henry Clinton was ordered to mount an amphibious expedition against Charleston. Ten British warships and more than thirty transports moored outside the city. But the people of Charleston were enraged and the city was mobilized to repel the "enemy." They tore down the warehouses along the waterfront to clear the range for cannon fire, and cut down palmettos to use as defense against British artillery. A contingent of North Carolina infantry came marching in to join the battle, and from Virginia came Reverend Peter Muhlenberg leading a well-equipped infantry regiment.

Commodore Sir Peter Parker ordered the British ships to fire, while the Redcoat infantry was being landed. But the palmetto logs absorbed the British fire, while the Rebel shore batteries ripped up the invading ships. The infantry was cut to pieces by Rebels commanded by Colonel William Moultrie, and the British fleet fled. Sir Peter, valiantly observing the destruction from the forward vessel, was himself wounded and thereafter required assistance in order to walk. The nature of his wound amused the Rebels, for according to one account his britches were "torn off, his backside laid bare, his thigh and knee wounded." Many songs were written, but this one (1776), ascribed humorously to Sir Peter himself, is one of the most printable.

*Sir Henry Clinton*

# Peter Parker

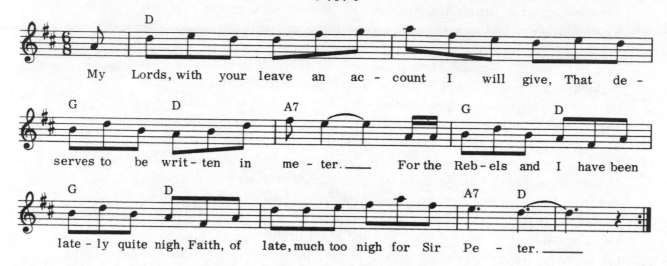

My Lords, with your leave an ac-count I will give, That deserves to be writ-ten in me-ter.___ For the Reb-els and I have been
late-ly quite nigh, Faith, of late, much too nigh for Sir Pe-ter.___

My Lords, with your leave an account I will give,
That deserves to be written in meter.
For the Rebels and I have been lately quite nigh,
Faith, of late, much too nigh for Sir Peter.

With much labor and toil unto Sullivan's Isle
I came, firm as a Falstaff or Pistol;
But the Yankee, 'od rot 'em, I could not get at 'em,
And they wrecked my flagship called the Bristol.

Devil take them, their shot came so swift and so hot,
And the cowardly dogs stood so stiff, sirs,
That I put ship about and was glad to get out,
Or they would not have left me a skiff, sirs.

Now bare as a stork I proceed to New York,
Where with Clinton and Howe you may find me,
I've the wind in my tail, and I'm hoisting my sail,
Leaving Charleston a long way behind me.

But, my Lords, never fear, for before the next year,
A new set of breeches we'll get us,
And we'll take, by my soul, this new continent whole,
(If the cowardly Yankees will let us.)

THE FINAL page of Tom Paine's inflammatory *Common Sense* carried one title that was both thrilling and frightening to the embattled Rebels—"The Free and Independent States of America." Even the most rebellious had hoped that good King George would reprimand his ministers and make peace with his loyal colonials. But Paine made a good case for an end to such optimism, calling the King, "The Royal Brute."

It was the King who really announced the separation between American colonies and British Government, when in 1776 he agreed to a Prohibitory Act. This forbade any intercourse with the colonies, and ordered a naval blockade to carry out this mandate. By May even the vacillating John Adams agreed that Independence "rolls in upon us . . . like a torrent." On June 7, the delegate from Virginia, Richard Henry Lee, offered a resolution to the Congress, "That these united colonies are and of right ought to be free and independent states."

More prudent delegates were fearful. The colonies had no foreign allies, an outstanding lack of munitions, and there was a powerful British navy and army preparing for an invasion. It didn't seem quite the time for flamboyant resolutions. Nevertheless on July 2, Thomas Jefferson's draft of a "Declaration of Independence" was adopted unanimously. Each delegate knew that his signature would be in British hands the next day, and that a victory for England would mean an immediate hanging. But they agreed, "For the support of this Declaration, with a firm reliance on the Protection of Divine Providence, we mutually pledge to each other our Lives, our Fortunes, and our sacred Honor."

They did not spare King George this time. After listing 27 paragraphs of "injuries and usurpations," the Declaration observed, "A Prince, whose character is thus marked by every act which may define a Tyrant, is unfit to be the ruler of a free People."

In some of its declarations, the document was more a guideline for the future than a plan for the present. The line, "We hold these truths to be self-evident" (which Franklin had changed from Jefferson's "We hold these truths to be sacred and undeniable"), was followed by the clause ". . . that all men are created equal"—this in a land where one-fifth of the population was enslaved, and many others were indentured workers—a form of economic thralldom.

The thrust of the Declaration was so inflammatory that it turned some fence-sitters into Tories. But it was also an inspiring document and was the beginning of hundreds of commentaries in prose and song. This song is the work of Dr. Jonathan M. Sewall of New Hampshire, adopted son of Chief Justice Stephen Sewall of Massachusetts Colony.

# Independence Day

Come, all you brave sol-diers, both val-iant and free. It's for In-de-
pend-ence we all now a-gree. The cause is so glo-ri-ous
we need not fear. From mer-ci-less ty-rants we'll set our-selves clear.

Come all you brave soldiers, both valiant and
    free,
It's for Independence we all now agree,
The cause is so glorious we need not fear,
From merciless tyrants we'll set ourselves clear.

Let's gird on our swords and prepare to defend,
Our liberty, property, ourselves, and our
    friends;
Still fighting we'll die in America's cause,
Before we'll submit to tyrannical laws.

George the Third of Great Britain no longer
    shall reign,
With unlimited sway o'er these free States
    again;
Lord North, nor old Bute, nor none of their
    clan,
Shall ever hold sway o'er an A-merican.

Upon our great Congress may Heaven bestow,
Both wisdom and skill our good cause to pursue;
On Heaven alone dependent we'll be
But from all earthly tyrants we mean to be
    free.

Unto our brave Generals may Heaven give
    skill,
Our armies to guide, and the sword for to
    wield;
May their hands taught to war and their fingers
    to fight,
Be able to put British armies to flight.

And now, brave Americans, since it is so,
We're now independent, we'll have them all
    know,
That united we are, and united we'll stand,
And keep British tyranny out of our land.

New music and edited text © 1972 by Oscar Brand

BENEDICT ARNOLD—this battered hero, anathema in American history, was about to embark on a course which would save the Revolution from a sudden demise. Arnold came from a good family, his great-grandfather had been Governor of Rhode Island, but his father was an alcoholic, and after a spotty apprenticeship as a druggist, the young man was forced to sell the old homestead in Norwich and moved to New Haven.

He opened a small druggist shop which, in the modern fashion, also carried a stock of books which extended his education. Prospering, he bought a ship and captained it himself through a number of voyages to the West Indies. His horse-trading took him to Montreal and Quebec, so that he was well-acquainted with these northern fortresses. He was in the West Indies when news of the Boston Massacre arrived. He wrote thereupon, "Good God, are the Americans all asleep, and tamely yielding up their liberties, or are they all turned philosophers, that they do not take immediate vengeance on such miscreants?"

In 1774, the popular Arnold, who had seen service with the British in the French and Indian War, was elected Captain by a local militia company. As soon as he heard of the battles at Lexington and Concord, he assembled his men and marched off to Cambridge. It was at his insistence that the Ticonderoga expedition had been mounted, although Ethan Allen garnered most of the glory. In recognition of his leadership qualities Congress appointed him a brigadier general, a fact which he learned only after he had been wounded during the defeat at Quebec.

Through his spies and scouts, Arnold learned that Sir Guy Carleton was mounting an offensive which, it was expected, would cut off New England from the rest of the colonies. There was nothing between Carleton in Canada and General Howe in New York except for Arnold and his men. The roads south were not passable, so Carleton decided to take his army by boat down Lake Champlain, through Lake George, and into the Hudson.

Somehow, Benedict Arnold organized a makeshift fleet—hammered together on the spot, with little armament, manned by soldiers with little experience in navigation or naval warfare. The foolish little navy confronted the mighty British fighting force on October 11, 1776, and was destroyed in two engagements. But Carleton and his force were so taken aback by the unexpected resistance that they neglected to advance further, and eventually withdrew to Canada.

Admiral Alfred T. Mahan, America's highly respected naval expert, has observed: "Never had any force, big or small, lived to better purpose, or died more gloriously." Arnold's tinderbox navy gave the colonies a year to prepare for the next invasion from Canada—led by General John Burgoyne.

The encounter proved one other fact—that the Rebels could hope for no French uprising in Canada. The few Canadians who came down to enlist in the Revolution were interested more in booty and in glory than in politics. This Canadian song, concerning the naiveté of a French-Canadian volunteer, is still sung in Quebec.

# The Little Sergeant

*Mon papa, si vous me battez, oui jirai m'engager,*
*A bord des Bostonnais, battre contre l'Anglais,*
*A Boston il s'en est alle', "How many men fired away?"*
*Voulez-vous m'engager pour un sergent guerrier?"*

Oh, father, if you will agree, then I will go and see,
If I can go and fight the British troops tonight.
To Boston he did make his way, "Are you in need of troops today?
A sergeant I would be. Sirs, will you hire me?"

Oh, yes, we will hire you to join our Rebel crew,
Although you're not too large, we'll let you lead the charge.
A sword and pistol at his side, his chest puffed out with manly pride,
He couldn't ask for more, he was a sergeant of the corps.

Then a British volley rang out, the charge became a rout,
And our little sergeant fell, for the British aimed too well,
But still and all he rose again,
And bravely called unto his men,
"Although your sergeant's shot, fight on and waver not!"

Our sergeant is home once again and bitterly doth complain,
When all is said and done, a battlefield is no fun,
His father wisely nods his head, "You'd best leave honor to the dead,
We Frenchmen should ignore their Anglo-Civil war."

*Benedict Arnold*

IT SEEMED clear that the British would soon attack New York and Long Island. The British Army was on the march and heavy reinforcements were expected daily by General Howe. New York was considered Tory territory although on July 9, 1776, its representatives had agreed to the Declaration of Independence. English and American Tories insisted that the British protect their New York brethren, and, since it fitted in with his military needs, Howe began to prepare his attack.

The Tories, meanwhile, were defending themselves against unruly mobs, and writing witty rhymes about the ridiculous "Declaration":

> After John Presbyter, Will Democrat came next,
> Who swore all men were even and seemed to be quite vext,
> That there's a king in heaven, and he curst the hills around,
> Because they made for unequal ground.

But the rhymes were no longer considered good clean fun. Nor were the Tories accepted as generally harmless political enemies. Even the old religion was suspected of treason. And as the quoted rhyme demonstrates, the Tories blamed mob rule and sedition on the new Presbyterian religion.

In New York especially, there was a strong division along religious lines. The Tories seemed to flock around the De Lanceys and the old Episcopal Church, while the revolutionaries sided with the Livingstons and the Presbyterian Church. Thus, when the British took control, the redcoats sometimes burned the Presbyterian churches, quartered among the pews, and often used the altars for firewood. The American militia returned the compliment by desecrating innumerable Congregational pulpits in appropriate profane and obscene manner.

The arrival of Washington and his army in New York further exacerbated the division. Washington heartily approved repressive measures as far as Tories were concerned. He applauded many intemperate actions against Americans suspected of sympathy with the British, and immediately announced, on his arrival, ". . . It is high time to begin with our internal foes when we are threatened with such severity of chastisement from our kind parent without."

The chastisement was carried aboard more than 500 ships which suddenly appeared out of the mists of Staten Island. Commanded by Admiral Richard Howe, General Howe's brother, jammed with some of England's finest soldiers and thousands of highly efficient German mercenaries, the British fleet arrived off New York Harbor in 1776. To add to this mighty force came Peter Parker's flotilla returning from the South with thousands of troops eager to wipe out the memory of the Charleston defeat.

It was the largest armed force ever seen in the New World—10,000 sailors and at last 25,000 well-trained magnificently-equipped soldiers. Some of these were singing a new tender ballad, "The Banks of The Dee." This had been written by John Tait, an Edinburgh judge, in 1775 on the departure of some friends to "quell the proud Rebels" in the colonies. It had become popular in England and among the soldiers abroad, and later provoked many Rebel parodies.

*The retreat from Long Island*

# The Banks of the Dee

'Twas summer and softly the breezes were
  blowing,
And sweetly the nightingale sang from the tree.
At the foot of a hill, where the river was
  flowing,
I sat myself down on the banks of the Dee.
Flow on, lovely Dee, flow on, thou sweet river,
Thy banks, purest stream, shall be dear to me
  ever,
For there I first gained the affection and favor,
Of Jamie, the glory and pride of the Dee.

But now he's gone from me and left me thus
  mourning,
To quell the proud Rebels, for valiant is he,
But ah! there's no hope of his speedy returning,
To wander again on the banks of the Dee.
He's gone, hapless youth, o'er the rude roaring
  billows,
The kindest, the sweetest, of all his brave
  fellows,
And left me to stray 'mongst these once-lovéd
  willows,
The loneliest lass on the banks of the Dee.

New music arrangement and edited text © 1972 by Oscar Brand

But time and my prayers may perhaps yet
  restore him,
Blest peace may restore my dear lover to me;
And when he returns, with such care I'll watch
  o'er him,
He never shall leave the sweet banks of the Dee.
The Dee then will flow, all its beauty displaying,
The lambs on its banks will again be seen
  playing,
Whilst I, with my Jamie, am carelessly straying,
And tasting again all the sweets of the Dee.

*General William Howe*

GENERAL HOWE'S orderly books are beautiful examples of flowery penmanship. One page is headed, "Headquarters, Staten Island, 20th August 1776," and announces the order of the day: "The Army will Land in four divisions, the first consisting of three Batteries, Lt. Infantry and the Reserve, under the Command of Lieut. Gen'l Clinton, Lt. Gen'l Earl Cornwallis, Maj. Gen'l Vaughan and Brig. Gen'l Leslie."

The British had complete control of the water. They could land men wherever the General deemed it necessary. They could harass the Rebels and cut off their supplies whenever they wished . . . unless Washington took up his positions on the far side of the Hudson River. To this day historians and military experts vie in attempting to exculpate Washington for his plan of battle. It is said that he was forced by political considerations to straddle the waterways. It is said that smallpox had deprived him of so many headquarters assistants that he was overburdened with details.

Nevertheless, Washington almost single-handedly lost the Revolution in New York. He split his forces unwisely and stationed an army on Long Island, an army on Brooklyn Heights, and an army in New York City. Howe had learned his lesson at Breeds' Hill, and refused to be lured into a frontal assault. He landed his men on Long Island, but instead of attacking the entrenched Rebels, his men marched around them and attacked in the rear. There was panic in the Rebel ranks. The marvelous rifles took too long to reload and were no good for hand-to-hand combat since they could not accommodate the necessary bayonets.

Retreat was ordered, giving Howe a marvelous opportunity to destroy the fleeing colonials. But perverse winds kept the British fleet out of the East River while the Army hurriedly took positions in the entrenchments on Brooklyn Heights. Washington now realized his error—he had to get his men across to New York or they would be caught between the powerful British soldiery and the guns of the British fleet. And he must do this without the British suspecting a withdrawal.

Washington called on the Massachusetts sailing men among his forces, ordered every viable boat commandeered, and for six hours quietly organized one of the most masterly evacuations in history. The next morning Howe discovered that almost 10,000 Rebels had been rowed out of his reach and were on Manhattan Island. Oh, well, thought Howe, the fleet was certainly ready to surround the Island and destroy the only colonial army in the field.

Clinton's Redcoats landed at Kip's Bay on September 15, and the American militia fled. Howe followed a little too slowly and Washington finally did what his officers had suggested many times, he took his army north to Westchester. All this time, the brothers Howe were carrying a message of peace from King George—pardon to relenting Rebels. But even though Ben Franklin, John Adams, and Edward Rutledge met with Howe, all knew that there was no chance of capitulation.

# A Parody of the Banks of the Dee

(SEE "*The Banks of the Dee*" FOR THE MUSIC)

'Twas winter and blue Tory noses were
   freezing,
As they marched o'er the land where they
   ought not to be,
The valiants complained of the fifers' curst
   wheezing,
And wished they'd remained on the banks of
   the Dee,
Lead on, thou paid captain! Tramp on, thou
   hired minions,
Thy ranks, basest men, shall be strung like ripe
   onions,
For here thou hast found heads with warlike
   opinions,
On the shoulders of nobles who ne'er saw the
   Dee.

Prepare for war's conflict, or make preparation,
For peace with the Rebels, for they're brave
   and glee,
Keep mindful of dying and leave the foul
   nation,
That sends out its armies to brag and to flee,
Make haste, now, and leave us, thou miscreant
   Tories,
To Scotland repair, and there court the sad
   houris,
And listen once more to their 'plaints and their
   stories,
Concerning the "glory and pride of the Dee."

Be quiet and sober, secure and contented,
Upon your own land, be there valiant and free;
Bless God, that the war is so nicely prevented,
And till the green fields on the banks of the
   Dee,
The Dee then will flow, all its beauty displaying,
The lads on its banks will again be seen playing,
And England thus honestly taxes defraying,
With natural drafts from the banks of the Dee.

New music arrangement and edited text © 1972 by Oscar Brand

*Cunningham destroying Nathan Hale's letters*

I N TOLLAND COUNTY, Connecticut, there is a house built in 1776 by the father of Nathan Hale. The father expected that the son would bring up his family in the house, would join the ministry, and, in general, comport himself in conservative fashion. Hale never saw the house. A month before the family moved into the completed dwelling, he was executed as a spy.

Hale was the poorest possible choice for the job for which he was chosen. He had never been a spy before, he was almost incapable of deception, and always eager to discuss his mission with fellow officers. Furthermore, he was not quite the faceless type that does well at espionage—Hale's face had been scarred by exploding powder and was not easy to forget. He had another characteristic which should have disqualified him—many of his relatives were Tories, and his cousin, Samuel Hale, was the British Army's deputy commissary of prisoners.

Hale was landed at Huntington, Long Island, and changed into a brown linen summer suit, having decided to do his spying under the guise of a Dutch schoolmaster. He carried his Yale diploma with him, but he decided to leave his silver shoebuckles behind realizing the British would know that a teacher's pay could never support such extravagance.

By the time Hale reached Long Island, the British had successfully marched into Manhattan, which meant that any information he might collect concerning the enemy on Long Island would be of little use. Most professional spies would have returned to Washington's headquarters. But Hale was a remarkably brave and dedicated man. As he wrote to his father, "A sense of duty urged me to sacrifice everything for my country." Hale, therefore, decided to spend his second week in Manhattan, where he observed British dispositions and wrote the information down neatly on his little note pad.

Hale should have been able to pass the material to Washington through "contacts," but none had been suggested to him. He should have been equipped with disappearing ink, a common espionage practice, but he had none and did not know how to make it. So he carried the incriminating note pad in the pocket of his plain brown linen suit, which is where the British found it. He had been walking on the East River shore, hoping that an American boat might come by, had hailed a small craft from the British ship *Halifax*, and was so disturbed when he realized his mistake that the British officer knew something was amiss.

Hale admitted his mission, and General Howe immediately ordered him to hang, turning him over to William Cunningham, his Provost Marshal. Cunningham was a cold-hearted man who was himself hanged for forgery in 1791 in London, but the reports of his cruelty to Hale have been much exaggerated. What is important is that the young man is said to have stood on the gallows and recited what experts say is a paraphrase of a line of Joseph Addison's, "What pity is it that we can die but once to serve our country!" Hale's words, recorded by Captain John Montresor, Chief Engineer of the British army, were: "I only regret that I have but one life to lose for my country!"

# Hale in the Bush

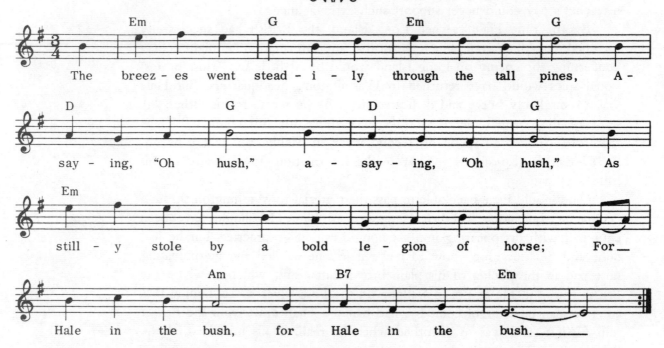

The breezes went steadily through the tall pines,  
A-saying, "Oh hush," a-saying, "Oh hush,"  
As stilly stole by a bold legion of horse;  
For Hale in the bush, for Hale in the bush.

He warily trod on the dry rustling leaves,  
As he pass'd through the wood, as he passed through the wood;  
And silently gained his rude launch on the shore,  
As she played with the flood, as she played with the flood.

The guards of the camp on that dark, dreary night,  
Had a murderous will, had a murderous will;  
They caught him and took him afar from the shore,  
To a hut on the hill, to a hut on the hill.

The brave fellow told them, no thing he restrained,  
The cruel general, the cruel general,  
His errand from camp and the ends to be gained,  
And said that was all, and said that was all.

Five minutes were given, short moments, no more,  
For him to repent, for him to repent;  
He prayed for his mother, he asked not another,  
To Heaven he went, to Heaven he went.

The faith of a martyr, the tragedy showed,  
As he trod the last stage, as he trod the last stage;  
And Britons will shudder at gallant Hale's blood,  
As his words do presage, as his words do presage.

THE WOUNDED Rebel Army retreated from New York with the British close after. And then Washington effected a classic maneuver— as the forward units of Howe's troops rushed ahead to attack the stragglers, they were cut off by flank attacks. The rebel attackers were units from Rhode Island, Massachusetts, Connecticut, Maryland, and Virginia, most of whom were veterans of the inglorious rout at Kip's Bay. The British were forced to retreat, and the news of this glorious surprise was carried through the colonies. Although the Rebels continued their withdrawal, north into Westchester, the world soon knew that a massive British offensive had been thrown back by an amateur army compounded of quasi-national units.

Throughout the war, the British opposition party found a certain amount of satisfaction in military reverses. As one British Tory observed, "The parricide joy of some in the losses of their country makes me mad." Continually, the conduct of the war was attacked for its unethical intentions and its incompetent direction. William Burke commented sourly, "No man commends the measures which have been pursued, or expects any good from those which are in preparation."

The Secretary of State for the Colonies, Lord George Germain, had been court-martialed for cowardice in 1760, having refused to participate in a cavalry charge. He had been declared "unfit to serve his Majesty in any military capacity whatsoever." He was now responsible for the conduct of the British Army in the colonies. The Earl of Sandwich, whose public debauchery was almost as scandalous as other ministers' private conduct, was First Lord of the Admiralty. When William Pitt heard the names of the officers who had been chosen to the Army command, he is said to have commented, "I do not know what effect these names have on the enemy, but I confess they make me tremble."

The following appropriate song was reportedly written in England in 1776 and transported to America. It demonstrates that the King was no longer excused for the poor quality of national policy.

# Song of the Heads

(SEE "*You Simple Bostonians*" FOR THE MUSIC)

Ye wrong heads, ye strong heads, attend to my
strains,
Ye clear heads, ye queer heads, ye heads without
brains,
Ye thick skulls, ye quick skulls, ye heads great
and small,
And ye heads that aspire to be heads over all,
CHORUS:
    Derry down, down, hey derry down.

Enough might be said, dared I venture my
rhymes,
On crowned heads and round heads of these
modern times,
This slippery path let me cautiously tread,
The neck else may answer, perhaps, for the
head.     CHORUS:

The heads of the church and the heads of the
state,
Have taught much and wrought much—too
much to repeat,
On the neck of corruption (uplifted, 'tis said),
Some rulers, alas, are too high by a head.
    CHORUS:

Expounders, confounders, and heads of the law,
I bring case in point, I do not point the flaw,
If reason is treason, what plea shall be pled?
To enable the pleader to maintain his head
    CHORUS:

On Britannia's bosom sweet Liberty smiled,
The parents grew strong while she fostered the
child;
Neglecting her offspring, a fever she bred,
Which contracted her limbs and distracted her
head.     CHORUS:

Ye learned state doctors, your labors are vain,
Proceeding by bleeding to settle her pain,
Much less can your art the lost members restore,
Amputation must follow—perhaps something
more!     CHORUS:

THE REBELS ON Long Island had ordered suspected Tories to take an oath of allegiance to the Cause. In 1776 the British Army was in control of the area, and the Tories came out of their hiding places, exulting in the happy reversal. They insisted that all suspected Rebels be required to take an oath of allegiance to the Crown, and they offered their services to the British Army as regulars, guerillas, or spies.

Howe began to enlist recruits from among the loyal colonials, and many of these slipped back and forth through Washington's lines carrying important information. One Tory recruiter behind the Rebel lines noted, "There was not much danger of being ketched, for the Torys had prepared private Cellars along the way." Washington was informed that, among his troops, were a British captain, a British lieutenant, two British sergeants, and countless Tory informers, but he was able to expose only a few.

The tall general became the target of anti-Rebel spite. The *New York Gazette* declared that the Rebel leaders were "obscure pettifogging attorneys, bankrupt shopkeepers, outlawed smugglers, wretched banditti," and one Tory statement described Washington as "the Great Captain of the western Goths and Huns."

The Tories worried Washington less than did the condition of his troops. From Haarlem Heights, he had written to the Congress, "We are now, as it were, upon the eve of another dissolution of our army. . . . It is in vain to expect that any more than a trifling part of this army will again engage in the service on the encouragement offered by Congress. When men find that their townsmen and companions are receiving twenty, thirty, or more dollars for a few months' service, which is truly the case, it cannot be expected, without using compulsion; and to force them into the service would offer no valuable purpose." Washington noted further that the officers were complaining bitterly as well: ". . . His pay will not support him, and he cannot ruin himself and family to serve his country."

Some of Washington's officers were willing to serve, but not swift to obey his commands. General Charles Lee, appointed by the Congress, refused an order to join the main body of the army when it fell back across the Hudson River. Luckily, he was captured by the British at such a distance from his own troops that they were able, unmolested, to join their compatriots. It is unlikely that any of the other generals could have commanded the respect that Washington was accorded by his men. The soldiers believed in him even in the bitter days of retreat.

# Follow Washington

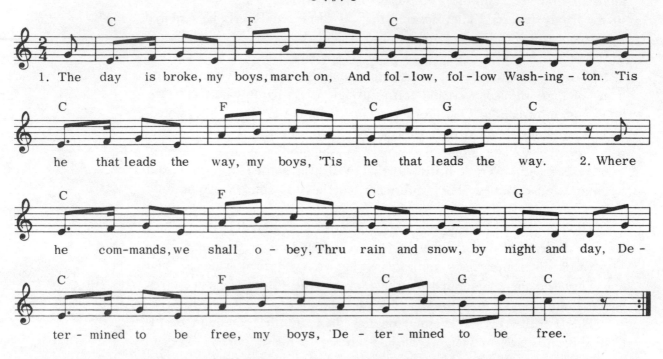

1. The day is broke, my boys, march on, And fol-low, fol-low Wash-ing-ton. 'Tis he that leads the way, my boys, 'Tis he that leads the way. 2. Where he com-mands, we shall o-bey, Thru rain and snow, by night and day, De-ter-mined to be free, my boys, De-ter-mined to be free.

The day is broke, my boys, march on,
And follow, follow Washington,
'Tis he that leads the way, my boys,
'Tis he that leads the way.

Where he commands we shall obey,
Through rain and snow, by night and day,
Determined to be free, my boys,
Determined to be free.

Till Freedom reigns our happy bands,
Will fight like true Americans,
Until our cause prevails, my boys,
Until our cause prevails.

With heart and hand, and God our trust,
We'll freely fight, our cause is just,
March on, my boys, my boys, march on,
And follow Washington.

New music and edited text © 1957 by Oscar Brand

AS WASHINGTON had observed, the army was facing dissolution at the end of the year, when enlistments ran out. He had to inspire his men, and quickly. The British had bedded down for the winter without fear of the mauled Rebels who had withdrawn across the Delaware and were freezing in Pennsylvania. Lord Cornwallis started packing for a rest in England. General Clinton was enjoying the pleasures of Newport, Rhode Island, and the key city of Trenton was garrisoned by the Hessian regiments, which had distinguished themselves during the recent battles at Fort Washington and Fort Lee.

The Hessians had also been distinguished for their pillaging and destruction of civilian houses and property. Ambrose Serle of Lord Howe's staff wrote in his journal, "It is impossible to express the Devastations which the Hessians have made upon the Houses and Country Seats of some of the Rebels. All their Furniture, Glasses, Windows, and the very Hangings of the Rooms are demolished or defaced. This with the Filth deposited in them, make the Houses so offensive, that it is a Penance to go into them."

Trenton, then, was a prime target, and a victory was necessary. As Washington noted, "Necessity, dire necessity, will, nay must, justify my attack." On January 1, the Army would consist of 1,400 men, and the army, at the moment, was the Revolution. All that was needed was a victory, and for that victory, Washington needed information. He cast about for a spy, "that we may, if possible, obtain some knowledge of the enemy's situation, movements and intentions. . . . We are in the neighborhood of very disaffected people, equal care therefore should be taken that one of these persons do not undertake the business in order to betray us."

In response to Washington's plea, John Honeyman of Griggstown set out to investigate the defenses in Trenton, declaring himself a knee-jerk Loyalist. His credentials were above suspicion, for, as a British soldier, he had carried the dying General Wolfe from the field at the Battle of Quebec. He also had a strong Scots accent, which was a passport to Tory confidence. However, Honeyman was part Irish, and it was to this he attributed his overwhelming love of independence from Britain.

As soon as he had enough information, Honeyman allowed himself to be captured by Rebel outposts. Taken to Washington, he delivered his information to the Commander-in-Chief and then "escaped" back to the British lines. There he excitedly reported to Colonel Johann Gottlieb Rall, the Hessian Commander, that Washington's army was in fearful condition, ready to mutiny, and hopelessly disorganized. Colonel Rall was pleased with the news and ordered a fine Christmas dinner.

Washington announced to his men that the watchword would be "Victory or Death!" Three military scouts who knew the area disguised themselves as farmers and moved stealthily in advance of the troops. Silently the army was ferried across the Delaware by the same New England fishermen who had saved them from capture in the retreats across the East River and the Hudson. Suddenly a Tory farmer caught sight of the tiptoeing army. Before they could stop him, he was on his way to Hessian headquarters. He sent his news in to the commandant via a subordinate and was thanked for his concern. But Colonel Rall continued to eat and put the note, unread, into his pocket. It was found there as he lay dying after the town was taken.

For years after John Honeyman was persecuted as a Tory and his family shunned. Then one day, after the peace was declared, a party of Continental officers, lead by George Washington himself, rode up to his house. In front of his astonished neighbors, the Commander-in-Chief extended the nation's gratitude for John Honeyman's invaluable and secret service to the Republic.

# The Ballad of Trenton

On Christ-mas Day in sev-en-ty-six, Our rag-ged troops with bay-o-nets fixed, For Tren-ton marched a-way, for Tren-ton marched a-way.____ The Del-a-ware see! The boats be-low! The light ob-scured by hail and snow, But no sign of dis-may, but no sign of dis-may.____

On Christmas day in seventy-six,
Our ragged troops with bayonets fixed,
For Trenton marched away.
The Delaware see! The boats below!
The light obscured by hail and snow,
But no sign of dismay, but no sign of dismay.

Our object was the Hessian band,
That dared invade fair freedom's land,
And quarter in that place.
George Washington he led us on,
Whose streaming flag in storm or sun,
Had never known disgrace, had never known
   disgrace.

In silent march we passed the night,
Each soldier panting for the fight,
Though quite benumbed with frost.
Greene, on the left, at six began,
The right was led by Sullivan,
Who never a moment lost, who never a moment
   lost.

Their pickets stormed, the alarm was spread,
That Rebels, risen from the dead,
Were marching into town.
They scampered here, they scampered there,
And some for action did prepare,
But soon their arms laid down, but soon their
   arms laid down.

Now, brothers of the Patriot bands,
Let's sing deliverance from the hands,
Of arbitrary sway.
And as our life is but a span,
Let's raise the tankard while we can,
And toast that glorious day, and toast that
   glorious day.

*The Battle of Trenton*

LORD GEORGE GERMAIN admitted that hopes of a swift end to the uprising in the colonies were blasted by "that unhappy affair at Trenton." Worse followed. Cornwallis, hearing of the defeat at Trenton, cancelled his trip to England and rushed from New York with an army of reinforcements. January 2, 1777, in the evening, his powerful force cornered Washington's ragged troops in Trenton, with the Delaware River preventing them from a swift retreat. Cornwallis confidently went to bed promising that he would "bag the fox" in the morning.

Cornwallis' outposts watched the steadily burning fires of the little colonial army through the night. But, as the dawn came up, that was all they could see—steadily burning fires. Even the few soldiers who had kept the campfires alive that night had fled to join their long-departed comrades. Washington's men had muffled the wheels and chains of their supply carts with rags, and had slipped around the British flank.

While Cornwallis was raging at this deception, the Rebels, heading for Princeton, smashed into his rear guard. In the wild melee, the British bayonets began to overpower the colonial troops. Then Washington appeared, like a living monument, riding into the British lines and rallying his men. The British began a retreat, and Washington, his men cheering behind him, shouted, "It's a fine fox chase, my boys."

When the fleeing Redcoats disappeared on the road back to Trenton, the Rebels turned on the small British garrison at Princeton. While collecting sorely needed arms and munitions stored there, Washington learned that a Redcoat garrison had taken over Nassau Hall at Princeton College and had vowed to fight unto death. The General ordered Captain Alexander Hamilton to bring up one of Henry Knox's captured cannons and to persuade the British garrison to surrender. Hamilton's first round tore through a portrait of George II in the College Prayer Hall. At this the red-coated resisters filed quietly out of Nassau Hall and surrendered.

Washington assumed that Cornwallis would be coming after him again furiously determined to wipe out the defeats at Trenton and Princeton. He ordered his men, as quickly as they could, to move up into the Morristown Hills. Cornwallis arrived too late to intercept this withdrawal, and the small, weary army was saved again. And this time they were withdrawing in triumph. They had engaged the fiercest fighting aggregation in the world, and they had beaten it back. Now they could with pride make fun of the British accent, the British uniform, and the British inferiority in battle.

# The Old Soldiers of the King

Since you all must have singing and won't be said, "Nay,"
I cannot refuse when you beg and you pray.
I will sing you a song (as a poet might say),
Of King George's old soldiers who ne'er run away.
CHORUS:
    We're the old soldiers of the King,
    And the King's own regulars.

At Lexington we met with Rebels one day,
We got ourselves up in our finest array,
Our heads bid us stand, and our hearts bid us stay,
But our legs were strong-minded and took us away.   CHORUS:

They fought so unfairly from back of the trees,
If they'd only fought open we'd have beat them with ease,
They can fight one another that way, if they please,
But we don't have to stand for such tactics as these.   CHORUS:

We marched into Princeton with fifes and with drums,
With muskets and cannons, with swords and with bombs,
This great expedition cost infinite sums,
But some underpaid Doodles they cut us to crumbs.   CHORUS:

Our general staff planned the Yankee's defeat,
With stealth we'd surprise them the next time we'd meet,
We marched, not expecting that we might be beat,
So the generals' plan of surprise was complete.   CHORUS:

'Tis true that we turned, but that shouldn't disgrace us,
We did it to prove that the foe couldn't face us,
And they've nothing to boast, it's a very plain case,
Though we lost in the fight, we came first in the race.   CHORUS:

[ 89 ]

AS THE CIVIL WAR progressed, Rebels and Loyalists increased their attacks upon each other. When General Howe was approaching Philadelphia, according to James Allen, a neutral observer, "a persecution of Tories (under which name is included every one disinclined to Independence . . .) began; houses were broken open, people imprisoned without any color of authority by private persons, and a list of 200 disaffected persons made out; who were to be seized, imprisoned and sent off to North Carolina."

It is surprising that the Rebels were able to stand against the Loyalist power. In Philadelphia, for instance, more than one-half the people were believed to be against independence. But one historian observed that the more influential Tories "disdained to enter into controversy with the noisy blustering and bellowing Patriots."

Another reason for the Rebel success was desperation. The Tory believed he could bide his time, expecting that the Crown would take care of fanatics. But the Rebel had to scramble, since hanging might reward his failure. He propagandized against the Loyalists with a bitter scorn, accusing them of stealing powder from American munitions stores, of smuggling flour to the British, and of sending horses to the Redcoats while Washington's officers walked.

General Washington himself often raised his voice against the Loyalists, observing that the country must guard against "the diabolical and insidious arts and schemes carried on by the Tories to raise distrust, dissensions, and divisions among us."

The divisions in the South were greater and more violent. General Nathaniel Greene deplored the bloodshed, observing, "The Whigs seem determined to extirpate the Tories and the Tories the Whigs. Some thousands have fallen in this way, in this quarter, and the evil rages with more violence than ever. If a stop cannot be put to these massacres the country will be depopulated in a few months more, as neither Whig nor Tory can live."

There are many songs that reflect the angry passions of the time and some of them survive today in England, Canada, and the United States. Versions of the following ballad are to be found wherever English is spoken and generally agree on the unhappy events described.

# Ye Sons of North Britain

Ye sons of North Brit-ain, — you that used to range, In
search of for-eign coun-tries, your for-tune to change; A-
mongst your great num-ber was Don-ald Mon-roe, A-
way to A-mer-i-ca he like-wise did go.

Ye sons of North Britain, you that used to
  range,
In search of foreign countries, your fortune
  to change;
Amongst your great number was Donald
  Monroe,
Away to America he likewise did go.

Two sons with his brother he left them to
  stay,
Because of their passage he could not then pay.
When seven long winters were over and gone,
They went to their uncle and begged to
  move on.

And when they had sailed o'er the fierce
  ocean wide,
They were fired at by Rebels upon every side;
There being two Rebels that lurked in the
  wood,
They fired their pistols where the two brothers
  stood.

You cruelest monsters, the dying boy said,
You have killed my elder brother, and soon
  I shall be dead,
O, cursed be the day we undertook to go,
And find our dear father, named Donald
  Monroe.

O, woe to my hands, what is this I have done?
O, cursed be my fate, I have murdered my son.
Is it you, my dear father? Then stand you
  close by,
For now I have seen you, contented I'll die.

Then Donald Monroe weeping sank to one
  knee,
O, merciful heaven, take pity on me;
In hopes we will meet on a far brighter shore,
Where brothers will murder their brothers no
  more.

[ 91 ]

*Old Cannon on the Delaware at Red Bank*

THE CIRCUMSTANCES of war rarely have a soothing effect on the nerves. For the British the Revolution was especially nervewracking. Britain was always fearful of invasion, privateers were always raiding her shipping, and spies were everywhere. The famed playwright, Pierre Augustin Caron de Beaumarchais, who created the immortal barber Figaro, was shuttling between France and London enjoying his dramatic ventures into espionage. On one hand he was settling a blackmail affair for French royalty—retrieving a chest of incriminating letters from a transvestite known as Chevalier d'Eon. On the other hand he was establishing a trading company in the West Indies, financed by the King of France, to buy and transport supplies to the Rebels.

The British secret service nervously watched Beaumarchais but could not arrest him lest they disturb the uneasy alliance with France. Besides, there were so many double agents that no one could be sure that a spy might be arrested at the very moment he was working for a friendly government.

In the States, feelings of security rose and fell, depending on the daily news from the battlefields. When Howe outgeneraled Washington at Brandywine, Tory recruiting rose to an all time high. Though Washington declared, "I shall continue to retreat before them so as to lull them into security," the fleeing Continental Congress must have wondered if the British weren't sufficiently secure.

As the British marched into Philadelphia, the Tories turned out in mobs and volunteered in large numbers for army service. Then Washington attacked the British forces at Germantown. News of the battle depressed Tory recruiting for a while but then it was learned that Washington's officers had lost the initiative while debating a minor tactical problem. Howe accepted his victory as a matter of course and allowed Washington to retreat to Valley Forge. The Tories began to relax.

But there was no rest for the British. Philadelphia was alive with Rebel spies, and every once in a while, the populace was roused into panic by rumors of a Rebel attack. It was for this reason that the Battle of the Kegs had such a profound effect. David Bushnell, of Saybrook, Connecticut, had invented a naval torpedo which had almost been successful when used against the British fleet in New York City. Now he had another idea—a seagoing mine.

On January 5, 1778, Bushnell and his assistants, with the blessing of General Washington, loosed a deadly flotilla of powder kegs, primed to explode on contact with the British ships moored in the Delaware River. When these strange objects were sighted, the news was shouted through the city of Philadelphia with alarm or rejoicing, depending on the political bent of the crier. That the response to the kegs was so inappropriate testifies to the frazzled nerves of the participants.

It was a great propaganda triumph for the Rebels and it prompted Francis Hopkinson, signer of the Declaration of Independence, in 1778 to write this very popular lampoon.

# The Battle of the Kegs

(SEE "*Arnold Is As Brave a Man*" FOR THE MUSIC)

Gallants, attend and hear a friend trill forth
    harmonious ditty,
Strange things I'll tell which late befell in
    Philadelphia city,
'Twas early day, as poets say, just as the sun
    was rising,
A soldier stood on a log of wood and saw a
    sight surprising.

As in amaze he stood to gaze, the truth can't
    be denied, sirs,
He spied a score of kegs, or more, come floating
    down the tide, sirs,
A sailor, too, in jerkin blue, this strange ap-
    pearance viewing,
First damned his eyes in great surprise,
Then said, there's mischief brewing.

The kegs must hold the Rebel bold packed up
    like pickled herring,
And they've come down to take the town in
    this new way of ferrying,
The soldier flew, the sailor, too, and scared
    almost to death, sirs,
Wore out their shoes to spread the news and
    ran till out of breath, sirs.

Now up and down, throughout the town,
Most frantic scenes were acted,
For some ran here and some ran there, and
    some ran quite distracted.
Some "fire" cried, which some denied, but
    said the earth had quakéd,
And girls and boys with hideous noise ran
    through the town half-naked.

Arise, arise, Sir Erskine cries, the Rebels,
    more's the pity,
Without a boat are still afloat and ranged
    before the city.
The cannons roar from shore to shore,
The small arms make a rattle,
Since wars began I'm sure no man e'er saw
    so strange a battle.

The fish below swam to and fro attacked from
    every quarter,
Why sure, thought they, the devil's to pay,
'Mongst folks above the water;
The kegs, 'tis said, tho strongly made of Rebel
    staves and hoops, sirs,
Could not oppose the powerful foes, the
    conquering British troops, sirs.

A hundred men, with each a pen, or more
    —upon my word, sirs,
It is most true—would be too few their valor
    to record, sirs;
Tho, facing guns the Redcoat runs too fast
    for Yankee legs, sirs,
We all can see his bravery subduing Yankee
    kegs, sirs.

New music arrangement and edited text © 1972 by Oscar Brand

THE BRITISH "Gentleman Johnny" Burgoyne was considered a model major general. He had fought his way up from a cornetcy (second lieutenant's rating) in France and in Spain, and had organized his expeditionary corps in America on lines that were remarkably efficient for the time. His officers were forbidden to strike or to swear at subordinates, and his men responded to his command with admirable efficiency.

Burgoyne conceived a plan which he presented in person to the War Office in London. He would lead an Army down from Canada while General Howe would drive up from New York to Albany. Their meeting would cut New England off from the rest of the colonies and end the Revolution. George III endorsed the plan with his own signature. In 1777, Burgoyne returned to Montreal to organize the march. A while later, the War Office received General Howe's plan to march to Philadelphia. George III agreed to this plan, too, although it contradicted the already accepted proposal drawn up by Burgoyne. Historians have offered as an excuse for Lord Germain and George III that they expected Howe to capture Philadelphia quickly and start north immediately. Burgoyne was informed of this change of plan, and even he accepted it.

Gentleman Johnny set out with a small navy, a field train of 42 cannon, about 6,500 regulars, some Canadians and Tories, and 400 Indians. Apprised that Indians were often associated with wartime atrocities, Burgoyne made a speech which was translated for his brightly painted allies by one of his French scouts: "Aged men, women, children, and prisoners must be held sacred from the knife or hatchet, even in actual conflict: and while you shall receive compensation for the prisoners you take, you shall be called to account for scalps." In the House of Commons, Edmund Burke likened Burgoyne's warning to a speech by a zookeeper, about to open the cages of the wild beasts, exhorting them "not to harm any man, woman, or child."

At first, things went well for Burgoyne. Fort Ticonderoga was taken without a siege, after his artillerymen managed to wrestle some cannons up to a height commanding the Fort. Swiftly the British pursued the fleeing Rebels. There was a frightful battle, which was broken off only when a regiment of German mercenaries suddenly marched up to turn the tide. After that the going was slow—through mosquito-infested swamps, virgin forest, choked ravines, and gauntlets of sharp-eyed Rebel riflemen.

Then an Indian brought into the British camp the scalp of lovely young Jane McCrea. Jane was the fiancée of Lieutenant David Jones, one of the few Tories who had marched down from Canada. She had been staying, for protection, with a cousin of British General Simon Fraser, one of Burgoyne's favorite officers. Burgoyne was horrified, but he couldn't arrest the culprit for fear of losing his Indian allies.

The death of Jane McCrea was one of the most powerful propaganda coups of the war for the Rebels. They exploited it in pamphlets, newspaper stories, and songs. The following ballad was probably written after the War, possibly by the poet Henry William Herbert.

# The Ballad of Jane McCrea

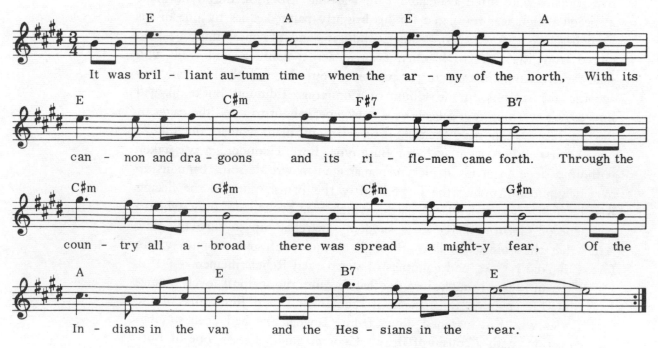

It was bril - liant au-tumn time when the ar - my of the north, With its can - non and dra - goons and its ri - fle-men came forth. Through the coun - try all a - broad there was spread a might-y fear, Of the In - dians in the van and the Hes - sians in the rear.

It was brilliant autumn time when the army
    of the north,
With its cannon and dragoons and its riflemen
    came forth.
Through the country all abroad there was
    spread a mighty fear,
Of the Indians in the van and the Hessians
    in the rear.

There was spread a mighty terror and the
    bravest souls were faint,
For the Indians were mustered in their scalps
    and in their paint,
And the forest was alive with the tramp of
    warrior men,
Scaring eagles from their nests and the gray
    wolf from his den.

For the Bold Burgoyne was marching with
    his thousands coming down,
To do battle with the people, to do battle for
    the Crown.
Johnny Stark stood by at Bennington by the
    Hoosic's waters bright,
Arnold waited with his forces gathered thick
    on Bemis height.

But a maiden fair lay weeping in her cottage
    day by day,
Tired was she, worn with watching for her
    true love far away.
He was bearing noble arms and crest, in service
    to the King,
While she waited sad and tearful near the pine
    tree, near the spring.

By the pine tree, near the spring, were arméd
    men, alert at post,
While the early sun was low'ring, watching
    for their royal host,
Came a rifle's sudden crack and rose a wild
    and fearful yell,
Rushed the Indians from the brake and fled
    the guard, or fought or fell.

Then a frantic savage seized her by her long
    and flowing hair,
Bared the keen and deadly knife and whirled
    aloft the tresses fair,
Yelled in triumph and retreated bearing off
    the trophy dread,
Think of him who sent them forth, and who
    received it, reeking red.

Now a little fountain wells out cool and clear
    beneath the shade,
Cool and clear as when beside it fell that young
    and lovely maid,
These bear witness for the story how upon
    that cruel day,
Beauty, innocence, and youth there died in
    hapless Jane McCrea.

*Burgoyne and the Indian Chiefs*

IT WAS 1777. After the generally discouraging actions in the New York State campaign, British General Burgoyne realized that he would need reinforcements quickly and sent a dispatch to New York City. In return, he received a code letter, which seemed meaningless unless one put a cutout mask shaped like a guitar over it: "Sir W. Howe is gone to Cheasapeake Bay with the greatest part of the Army. I hear he is landed, but am not certain. I am left here with too small a force to make any effectual diversion in your favor. I shall try something at any rate." It was signed by General Henry Clinton, who had been left in charge of the British in New York.

Burgoyne decided to follow his original plan, anyway, and turned for advice to a local Loyalist, Major Philip Skene, who had fought in the French and Indian War. Burgoyne should have traveled by boat, but Skene advised him to build roads and march to Bennington where, he claimed, hordes of eager Tories would swell his army to unconquerable proportions. Skene had an unsavory reputation—it was believed that he kept the corpse of his mother in the parlor in order to collect her annuity, paid as long as she was "above ground." His advice seemed to be based mainly on his desire to have the British construct roads through his widely spread farmlands.

At Burgoyne's orders, a British force under General Barry St. Leger marched in from the west with a thousand troops and some 1,000 Indians. Major General Benedict Arnold was sent to meet them with less than 1,000 men. But Arnold sent pretended deserters ahead with the news that he was leading a tremendous army, and Burgoyne's Indians deserted. In fact, when St. Leger retreated before the imagined superiority of Arnold, his former Indian allies turned against him and attacked his rear guard.

Brigadier General John Stark led 2,000 volunteer New Hampshiremen against Burgoyne's Hessians and destroyed them at Bennington, Vermont. At the time, New Hampshire was not one of the rebelling colonies, but the soldiers fought as colonists nonetheless.

Without his Indian scouts, Burgoyne was blind, whereas the American commander in the region, Horatio Gates, had the help of volunteer secret servicemen who ranged back and forth through the lines. One of the best of these men was Alexander Bryan, who is rarely mentioned in historical accounts. General Gates promised Bryan that, if the scout would discover Burgoyne's battle plans, a medical officer would be dispatched to Bryan's home, where one of his sons was sick and his wife was near her confinement.

When Bryan returned with a complete list of British orders of battle, guns, horse and even the date of the attack against the American forces, he discovered that his son was dead and his wife was dying. Gates apologized for not sending the promised doctors, explaining that his troops needed all the medical help he could muster.

With Bryan's information in hand, the Rebels were more than ready for Burgoyne's attack. Their fortifications had been skillfully planned by the brilliant Polish engineer, Tadeusz Ardrzej Bonawent Kosciuszko, and their leaders included the most battle-wise veterans of the Revolution: Daniel Morgan and his riflemen, Enoch Poor's New Englanders, and the indefatigable Benedict Arnold. Burgoyne finally retreated to Saratoga, battered, harassed, and hopeless. When his German mercenaries refused to continue the profitless campaign, he surrendered his remaining troops.

According to one historical account, Burgoyne greeted General Gates with a salute, "The fortune of war, General Gates, has made me your prisoner," and Gates replied, "I shall always be ready to bear testimony that it has not been through any fault of your Excellency." But a survivor of the battle, Samuel Downing, swears that Burgoyne observed, "Are you a general? You look more like a granny than you do like a general." And Gates replied, "I be a granny, and I've delivered you of ten thousand men today."

*One of Morgan's Riflemen*

# Burgoyne's Defeat

Here fol-low-eth the dire—— fate Of Bur-goyne and his ar-my great, Who so proud-ly did dis-play The ter-rors of des-pot-ic sway. His pow-er, pride and man-y threats are now brought low by Gen-'ral Gates, To bend to the U-nit-ed States. Brit-ish pris-'ners by Con-ven-tion. *(Spoken freely) (Two thousand four hundred and forty-two.)* For-eign-ers by Con-tra-ven-tion. *(Spoken freely) (Two thousand one hundred and ninety-eight.)*

Here followeth the dire fate
Of Burgoyne and his army great,
Who so proudly did display
The terrors of despotic sway.
His power, pride, and many threats
Are now brought low by General Gates,
To bend to the United States.
British prisoners by Convention . . . . . . . 2,442,
Foreigners by Contra-vention . . . . . . . . . 2,198,
Tories sent across the Lake . . . . . . . . . . 1,100,
Burgoyne and his suite, in state . . . . . . . . 12,
Sick and wounded, bruised and pounded,
Ne'er so much before confounded . . . . . 528,
Prisoners before Convention . . . . . . . . . . . 400,
Deserters with benign intention . . . . . . . 300,
Lost at Bennington's great battle,
Where glorious Stark firearms did rattle 1,220,
Killed in September and October . . . . . . . 600,
Taken by Brown, some drunk, some sober 413,
Slain by far-famed Herkerman,
Upon both flanks, and rear and van . . . . 300,
Settler, Indian, and drover,
Enough to crowd the plain all over,
And those whom grim Death did prevent,
From fighting 'gainst our continent,
And also those who stole away,
And down their arms did choose to lay,
Abhoring that obnoxious day . . . . . . . . . 4,413,
The whole make fourteen thousand men,
Who may not with us fight again . . . 14,000.

*General Gates*

New music and edited text © 1972 by Oscar Brand

*Franklin at the French Court*

BURGOYNE'S SURRENDER at Saratoga was of momentous importance to the Rebels. Lord North immediately began preparing an offer of peace and sent secret emissaries to talk to the American commission in France, which was composed of Benjamin Franklin, Silas Deane, and Arthur Lee. The commissioners acquired exalted status upon the news of the victory, reporting that the French reacted with as much joy "as if it had been a Victory of their own Troops over their own Enemies." The French court especially applauded the duplicity of the Americans who first promised to release the British, but instead held them prisoner until the end of the war. This proved to the King's ministers that the new nation had learned the intricate business of international diplomacy.

King Louis XVI decided to postpone an alliance, however, until the King of Spain agreed to join. King Charles of Spain felt that he would rather wait until Britain was a little weaker. Franklin saw the chance of a French alliance disappearing, and resolved to convince the French in one of his usual subtle and clandestine intrigues. Knowing that French spies watched him ceaselessly, he invited the British emissary to his study. There he learned that Britain wanted peace but was not prepared to accept American independence. He dismissed the emissary.

Franklin, up to this moment, had been reporting his activities to the French ministry. This time he carefully neglected to mention that he had spoken to a British courier. The next day the Commissioners were visited by Conrad-Alexandre, Gerard de Rayvenal, 1st Secretary of the French Foreign Ministry. His first question was, "What is necessary to be done to give such satisfaction to the American Commissioners as to engage them not to listen to any propositions from England?"

The Treaty of Alliance, which was the answer to this question, was drawn up by Franklin and was daring in its provisions. It agreed to continue aiding the Rebels until the war was won, and to found "The Advantage of Commerce solely upon reciprocal Utility, and the just Rules of free Intercourse." France renounced any claims on land east of the Mississippi, and the United States guaranteed and France agreed to defend her present positions in the West Indies and any others she might conquer. And, since Franklin had always wanted to include Bermuda and Canada in the American nation, it allowed the new country to conquer them if she could.

With the new French ally, the Rebels would no longer feel helpless in the face of the marauding British fleet. And the recognition of their right to nationhood brought the colonies closer together. It also depressed the Tory cause in America, and was not much comfort for the Tories in Britain. Yet they did not give up, but bravely continued their efforts to save the Rebels from their own folly, as well as from alliances with Britain's own enemies, writing treatises, polemics, and inspirational songs, such as the following of 1779.

# Rouse, Britons

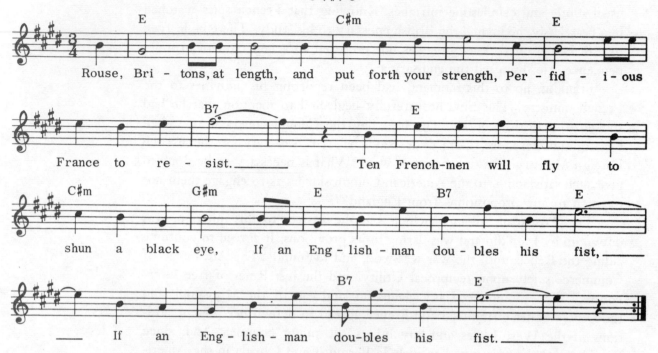

Rouse, Bri - tons, at length, and put forth your strength, Per - fid - i - ous
France to re - sist._____ Ten French-men will fly to
shun a black eye, If an Eng - lish - man dou - bles his fist,_____
_____ If an Eng - lish - man dou - bles his fist._____

Rouse, Britons, at length, and put forth your
   strength,
Perfidious France to resist,
Ten Frenchmen will fly to shun a black eye,
If an Englishman doubles his fist,
If an Englishman doubles his fist.

For their Dons and their ships we care not
   three skips
Of a flea—and their threats turn to jest, O,
We'll bang their bare ribs for their infamous
   fibs,
Which they cram in their fine manifesto,
Which they cram in their fine manifesto.

Our brethren so frantic across the Atlantic,
Who quit their old friends in a huff,
In spite of their airs are at their last prayers,
And of fighting have had quite enough,
And of fighting have had quite enough.

So if powers at a distance should offer as-
   sistance,
Say boldly, "We want none, we thank ye."
Old England's a match—and more—for Old
   Scratch,
A Frenchman, a Spaniard, a Yankee,
A Frenchman, a Spaniard, a Yankee.

New music and edited text © 1972 by Oscar Brand

*Lafayette*

WHILE THE Commission was negotiating with the French, Washington was wintering at Valley Forge, Pennsylvania. His reputation was at its lowest ebb, while General Gates was exceedingly praised for his Saratoga victory. Washington's favorite aide, the Marquis de Lafayette reported, "There are open dissensions in Congress, parties who hate one another as much as the common enemy: men who, without knowing anything about war, undertake to judge you and to make ridiculous comparisons. They are infatuated with Gates."

The end of the year, as usual, would mean the end of the terms of enlistment for one-third of the Rebel army. Compulsory military service had been instituted, but as in Rhode Island, the Assembly passed a law excusing those who swore, "I,————, do sincerely affirm and declare that the art of war and fighting . . . is utterly inconsistent with my belief as a Christian . . ." This led to a general manifestation of draft-age piety, so that two months later, the Assembly required those who were granted exemption to hire substitutes. Many Quakers and suspected Loyalists were tarred and feathered and soldiers were quartered in their homes as retaliation for their refusal to join the war effort.

Washington's men lacked food, ammunition, and clothing. He reported to Congress that he had been unable to attack a vulnerable British troop because, "The men were unable to stir on account of provision, and a dangerous mutiny, begun the night before . . . was suppressed by the spirited exertions of some officers."

Washington ordered General Gates to send the major portion of the victorious Saratoga army to Pennsylvania, together with captured paraphernalia of war. Gates was busy arranging for his promotion to Washington's job, and ignored the order. The little army was pleased to hear that Congress had decreed a Thanksgiving Day until the extra rations were meted out—half a gill of rice and a tablespoonful of vinegar. Continental soldier Joseph Plumb Martin wrote in his diary, "My companions . . . might be tracked by their blood upon the rough frozen ground. But hunger, nakedness, and sore shins were not the only difficulty we had at that time to encounter: we had hard duty to perform and little or no strength to perform it with."

Washington kept his men busy with the "hard duty." One of these duties was learning military drill, and the officer in charge was Baron Friedrich Wilhelm Ludolf Gerhard Augustin von Steuben, self-acclaimed drillmaster for Frederick the Great, self-appointed Lieutenant General of Infantry. His title was a fraud, his rank was a deception, and his vaunted service for the great Prussian Army was an ignoble exaggeration. But he knew the routine of the drill and he could swear in three languages. The winter at Valley Forge was a dreadful time, but when it was over, the Continental Army had been drilled by Von Steuben into a tough, trained aggregation of skilled soldiers. The day of the Doodle was over.

*Baron Steuben*

# Come Out, Ye Continentalers

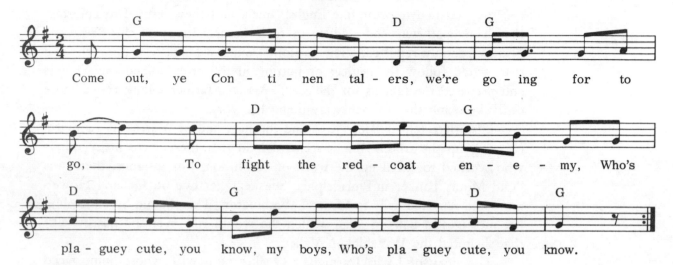

Come out, ye Con - ti - nen - tal - ers, we're go - ing for to go, ___ To fight the red - coat en - e - my, Who's pla - guey cute, you know, my boys, Who's pla - guey cute, you know.

Come out, ye Continentalers, we're going for
    to go,
To fight the Redcoat enemy,
Who's plaguey cute, you know, my boys,
Who's plaguey cute, you know.

First, shoulder WHOOP, eyes right
    DRESS FRONT,
Don't you twitch your nose,
Port WHOOP, that's good, now carry
    WHOOP,
Now all turn in your toes, my boys,
Now all turn in your toes.

Now bayonet FIX, that's fine, my men,
Now quicktime MARCH, that's right,
That's how we'd chase the enemy,
If he were but in sight, my boys,
If he were but in sight.

HALT, shoulder WHOOP, stop laughing
    there,
By columns, WHEEL, HALT, DRESS!
Hold up your muzzles on the left,
No talking more or less, my men,
No talking more or less.

Ho, strike up MUSIC, forward MARCH,
The Redcoats are in sight,
Now, bayonets FIX, and CHARGE, my men,
We'll show them how we fight, my men,
We'll show them how we fight.

THE ANTIQUE history of war is often a recital of masculine supremacy. But from the earliest days of the Rebellion, colonial housewives participated to a remarkable degree. They refused to brew the British tea, they refused to wear fine English linen, and they refused to entertain British sympathizers and soldiers in their homes. In 1776, the *Freeman's Journal* proudly reported, "The patriotic young women, to prevent the evil that would follow the neglect of putting in the crop, joined the ploughs and prepared the fallows for the seed." Many a farmer-soldier rested more easily knowing that women were doing his work.

Historians tell of Betsy Ross and the flag, and of Martha Washington cheering up the troops. But it seems certain that there were many others who worked to speed up the work of revolution. For instance, there was "Old Mom" Rinker in Philadelphia. She kept her eye on General Howe's army and reported daily to General Washington. This she did by concealing her messages in balls of yarn, which she would roll over the nearby cliff that sheltered the Wissahickon Valley.

The story of Lydia Darragh, a Quaker housewife whose home faced the front door of British Headquarters in Philadelphia, is an example of a woman who made an invaluable contribution to the Cause. She sewed her information into cloth-covered buttons which her fourteen-year-old son secretly delivered to General Washington. Washington read the information from Philadelphia eagerly, trying to extract from the outpouring of information the vital hints of General Howe's next move.

One night a group of British officers took over Mrs. Darragh's back room and ordered the family to go to bed early. For Lydia Darragh, this was a manifest invitation to eavesdrop. Thus she heard the decision to attack the weakened colonial army within two days' time. The next morning she set out to inform Washington of the British plan. Washington's intelligence officers began to analyze the information and decided that Howe would pretend he was retreating to New York, but would then cross the Delaware and attack the unguarded rear echelons of the Continental Army. They pointed out to the Commander-in-Chief that the British were building boats in the Delaware and it seemed obvious that an attack across the Delaware was planned.

Washington read Mrs. Darragh's information differently. He ordered his front lines strengthened, expecting a British frontal assault. He was right. The British marched forth feigning a march toward the Schuykill, swung around to hit the Americans, and then discovered that they were facing a powerfully reinforced Rebel army. After a few probing skirmishes, the entire British force swung around again and marched with injured dignity back into Philadelphia. When Cornwallis reported the affair to London, he added that, in his opinion, the Americans could never be conquered. His statement was a tribute to the female patriots who had wrecked his plans.

# The Female Patriots

All hail, su-pe-ri-or sex, ex-alt-ed fair,___ Mir-rors of vir-tue Heav-en's pe-cu-liar care,___ Ac-cept the tri-bute of our warm-est praise,___ The sol-dier's bless-ing and the pa-triot's bays.___

All hail, superior sex, exalted fair,
Mirrors of virtue, Heaven's peculiar care,
Accept the tribute of our warmest praise,
The soldier's blessing and the Patriot's bays.

No more sit weeping o'er the veteran band,
Those noble brave protectors of her land,
For lo, these sons her glorious work renew,
Cheered by such gifts, and smiles, and prayers from you.

Yes, now ye sister angels of each state,
Who cause our hearts to glow with joy elate,
For fame's first plaudit we no more contest,
Constrained to own it decks the female breast.

And so the future bards shall soar sublime,
And waft you glorious down the stream of time,
And freedom's ensign thus inscribed shall wave,
"The Patriot females who their country save."

New music and edited text © 1972 by Oscar Brand

IN DECEMBER 1777, Washington wrote to Congress, "Unless some great and capital change suddenly takes in that line, this army must inevitably be reduced to one or other of these things; starve, dissolve, or disperse." There was no change until May 6, 1778, when the French Alliance was announced to the troops. But it was not received with wholesome relief. The rebel coalition included hosts of Jews, Protestants, and agnostics, for whom an alliance with an entire Papist nation was an uncomfortable accommodation.

The Loyalists took advantage of this prejudice and began to turn out reams of pamphlets and poems on the subject, such as this quatrain from Rivington's *Gazette:*

> The French Alliance now came forth,
> The Papists flocked in shoals, sir,
> Friseurs, Marquis, Valets of Birth,
> And priests to save our souls, sir.

It was rumored in the ranks that the French fleet was on the high seas loaded down with crucifixes, rosaries, and indulgences, and that more cargoes of wafers, relics, and beads were being prepared. Even worse, it was reported that vats of scented soups, dried garlic and precooked frog's legs had been packed ready for immediate shipment to the colonies.

Nor was this the only subject for Tory diatribes. They were delighted to hear that even General Washington wasn't secure in his commanding position. Congress, it seemed, was becoming more and more convinced that General Charles Lee had the makings of a superior Commander-in-Chief. Lee had been returned by the British after his capture during the Hudson compaign. While a captive, Lee had spent his time working out effective campaigns for either side. When Congress ignored his plans—forwarded from his prison in the British camp—he submitted his counter-proposals to the enemy in the hope that they, at least, would recognize his military genius. The British High Command rejected Lee's plan, which promised to extinguish the rebellion "in less than two months." It may have been with a sense of relief that the British released General Lee.

Changing commanders in wartime was not unusual. General Howe, for instance, was recalled to England to explain his inactivity, leaving General Sir Henry Clinton in command. Clinton, hearing that a French fleet was heading for New York, decided to rush there in order to preserve his New York garrison. This meant that he would have to abandon Philadelphia, and the Loyalists in that city were loud in their complaints.

On June 18, 1778, Washington's spies informed him that Clinton was on his way to New York. General Charles Lee demanded the right to lead the attack, and Washington agreed. Lee issued a series of confusing orders, seemed to become disoriented himself, and finally ordered a retreat. At this point Washington rode up, treated Lee to a description of himself in terms worthy of an ox-driver, and took over the command.

But it was too late. When the Battle of Monmouth was over the Americans held the field, but Clinton's army was intact and on its way to New York. He arrived only a few days before the French fleet appeared off the coast. The Loyalists accelerated their campaign to show that the King was benevolent and all-forgiving, that Washington would be better off without his capricious Congress, and that Frenchmen made untrustworthy allies. That was the substance of the following song, probably written by James Rivington, the leading Tory spokesman, and printed in his *Royal Gazette* in October 1778.

*French Soldiers*

# The Farce

(SEE *"You Simple Bostonians"* FOR THE MUSIC)

The farce is now finished, your sport's at an
  end,
But ere you depart, let the voice of a friend,
By way of a chorus, the evening crown,
With a song to the tune of a "hey derry
  down,"
CHORUS:
  Derry down, down, hey derry down.

Old Shakespeare, a poet who should not be
  spit on,
Although he was born in the island called
  Britain,
Hath said that mankind are all players at best,
A truth we'll admit of, for sake of the jest.
                CHORUS:

On this puny stage we have strutted our hour,
And acted our parts to the best of our power,
That the farce hath concluded not perfectly
  well,
Was surely the fault of the devil in Hell.
                CHORUS:

The devil, you know, out of spleen for the
  church,
Will often abandon his friends in the lurch,
And turn them adrift in the midst of their joy,
'Tis a difficult matter to cheat the old boy.
                CHORUS:

Let Washington now from his mountain
  descend,
Who knows but in George he may yet find
  a friend,
A Briton, although he loves bottle and wench,
Is an honester fellow than *"Parlez vous
French."*              CHORUS:

Our great Independence we give to the wind,
And pray that Great Britain may once more
  be kind,
In this jovial song all hostility ends,
And Britons and we will forever be friends.
                CHORUS:

Once more, here's a health to the King and
  the Queen,
Confusion to him, who in rancor and spleen,
Refuses to drink with an English good friend,
Immutable amity to the world's end. CHORUS:

THE MILITARY alliance with France was soon productive. In 1778 a
French fleet consisting of twelve battleships and six frigates, commanded by Admiral Jean Baptiste d'Estaing, arrived off the American coast.
D'Estaing had served as Brigadier General in the Seven Years' war, and had
been captured by the British. When he returned, he was transferred to the

navy and appointed Vice Admiral, filled with an almost overwhelming urge to revenge himself and his country for humiliations suffered at the hands of the British. Arriving with 4,000 crack French troops at Sandy Hook, D'Estaing decided to attack, but American pilots warned him that his battleships were too heavy to pass over the sandy bar.

The French were under orders to spend only a short time with Washington before sailing to attack the British in the West Indies. D'Estaing hurriedly agreed with Washington on a plan to capture Newport, Rhode Island. He was to be aided by a land force commanded by General John Sullivan, presently in charge of a small army in Providence. Lafayette would join him with two brigades, and a Negro regiment was to march in, commanded by General Christopher Greene.

The combined attack went too well. British General Piggott, afraid that he would be surrounded, withdrew his 6,000 troops from the island, leaving a fine line of entrenchments. Sullivan, happily taking advantage of his good luck, moved his men in a day earlier than agreed. D'Estaing was horrified at this breach of proper military deportment and communicated his annoyance to the new French ambassador, Conrad-Alexandre Gérard de Rayvenal.

Just as the matter was being smoothed out and hot tempers were cooling, lookouts sighted the British fleet under Lord Richard Howe. The wind was with the British, while D'Estaing's ships could hardly maneuver in the narrow harbor. With victory in his grasp, Howe decided to give his men the night off so that they could better destroy the helpless French fleet. The next morning the French sailed out of the harbor in time to form a formidable battle line. The wind shifted in their favor, and Howe began to maneuver and fall back. D'Estaing began to maneuver and edge forward.

Constantly tacking and shifting about, the two fleets drifted out to sea—right into an Atlantic hurricane. By the time they recovered, battered and almost completely disabled, neither was in any condition to fight. D'Estaing was reminded of his original orders and, after a short stay in Boston to make necessary repairs, set off to the West Indies. This left the expeditionary force under Sullivan in an impossible position in Newport.

Luckily the colonial army included a detachment of the same Massachusettsmen who had saved the army so many times before. Again they bent to the oars and rowed the Rebels out of danger. Once again the Tory press had a subject for satire, and, once again, Rivington's *New York Gazette* printed a song which cleverly exploited the situation.

# The Affair at Newport

(SEE "*Arnold Is As Brave a Man*" FOR THE MUSIC)

From Louis, Monsieur Gérard came to Congress in this town, sir,
They bowed to him and he to them and then they all sat down, sir,
Begar, said Monsieur, one grand coup you shall *bientot* behold, sir,
This was believed as gospel true and Jonathan felt bold, sir.

So Yankee Doodle did forget the sound of British drums, sir,
How oft it made him quake and sweat in spite of Yankee rum, sir,
He took his wallet on his back, his rifle on his shoulder,
And vowed Rhode Island to attack before he was much older.

What numbers bravely crossed the seas I cannot well determine,
A swarm of Rebels and of fleas and every other vermin,
As Jonathan so much desired to shine in martial story,
D'Estaing with politesse retired to leave him all the glory.

He left him what was better yet, at least it was more use, sir,
The sample of a quick retreat, a very good excuse, sir,
To stay, unless he ruled the sea, he thought would not be right, sir,
And Continental troops, said he, on islands should not fight, sir.

EVEN BEFORE the Revolution, the western settlers had disobeyed the King's commands. The British Ministry had ordered an end to the movement westward in order to save money on troops, but there were many who echoed the frontier code, "When you see the smoke from a neighbor's chimney, it's time to move out." At first, the Indians welcomed the newcomers—after all, the Indian way of life allowed for no personal ownership of land. But the settlers had a different code, and they cleared the land, fenced the farms, and drove off "intruders."

In western Pennsylvania, in West Virginia, and in Daniel Boone's Kentucky, angry Indians tried to force the settlers back. When the War began they acquired an important ally. The representative of Britain in Detroit was Lieutenant Colonel Henry Hamilton, known as "The Hair Buyer." It was he who suggested to the frontier tribes that they secure scalps of colonial settlers which could then be traded in for rum, ammunition, blankets, arms and clothing. Kentucky became known as "The Dark and Bloody Ground."

About the time the French fleet was heading for the West Indies, George Rogers Clark set out to pacify the western Indians. His expedition was financed by the Virginia House of Burgesses, which was under the impression that Clark intended only to defend Kentucky against the Indians. But Clark was after bigger game—the fortress of Detroit and the Hair Buyer himself. The big Virginian's skill as a diplomat has rarely been matched. Meeting with tribe after tribe he smoked peacepipe after peacepipe to ensure that his men would be unmolested on the long march to Detroit. He was further able to convince the French traders and settlers that they would have freedom of religion and commerce under the auspices of the new nation. One town after another renounced the Crown, including the vital settlement of Vincennes. When Hamilton learned that his domain was in danger he set out for Vincennes with a small force of Tories, French militiamen, and Indians.

Hamilton's march was as remarkable as had been Clark's trek through the wilderness. Surprising the tiny garrison Clark had left in Vincennes, he took back the town, which impelled most of the French settlers in the territory to reaffirm their loyalty to King George. It was considered impossible, even in Spring, to traverse the swamps and rivers, the tangled timberlands, and the brambled brushwoods of the West. Now it was winter. Clark decided that Hamilton would be surprised if anyone attempted to make the impossible journey to Vincennes. Therefore, he made it, and Hamilton was indeed surprised. Clark used another stratagem to win the fort. He marched his tiny force through the town banging drums, singing, shouting, and announcing his superior numbers.

Believing in Clark's self-proclaimed superiority, the French inhabitants again forswore the Crown. Hamilton's Indians quit on the spot. Clark had one more surprise up his sleeve—he ordered a frontal assault on the well-manned fort, even though he was outnumbered by the defenders. His rifle men wasted few shots, and after watching his men being picked off one by one, the Hair Buyer surrendered. Clark hadn't taken Detroit, but he had made life easier for the western settlers, whose fighting songs thereafter had a brighter lilt to them.

# The Indian's Over the Border

Come, frontier men, awake now,
By mountain and by lake now,
And make the mountain shake now
With rifles' wild alarms,
For the red men come in swarms,
So frontier men to arms.

CHORUS:
  The Indian's over the border,
  The Indian's over the border,
  Prepared for pillage and slaughter,
  Come, frontier men, to arms.

From field and forest we come now,
To sounds of the horn and the drum now,
Prepare to fight for your home now,
In danger and alarm,
For the whoops and yells resound,
Then gather at the sound.        CHORUS:

We swear to know no rest, boys,
Until with peace we're blest, boys,
Until we've cleared the West, boys,
From danger's wild alarms,
Our cause each true heart warms,
Then frontier men to arms.        CHORUS:

New music and edited text © 1972 by Oscar Brand

BOTH SIDES courted the American Indian, hoping to make use of his skills in the art of war and his ancient knowledge of the countryside. Congress empowered Washington to raise a force of 2,000 Indians to augment his pitifully small army, but it wasn't easy cajoling the red chiefs into the Rebel camp. Most of the tribes honored their treaties of allegiance to the Crown and respected the British military forces. Besides, the Rebels were obviously interested in settling on Indian land, whereas the British were content with trading. Consequently, the Loyalist forces were well served by Indian allies.

The Iroquois Indians, before the Revolution one of the most powerful confederacies in America, were torn apart by divided loyalties. Urged on by missionary fervor, the Oneidas and many of the Algonquian Indians fought on the Rebel side. Members of their own tribes fought against them, joining the Senecas, Mohawks, and Cayugas led by legendary heroes such as Joseph Brant. It may seem strange to call Brant a hero, since his Indian forces have been described in envenomed prose in most historical accounts. However, Indian warfare was not expected to be the aboriginal equivalent of military chivalry. For great Indian generals such as Sayenqueraghta or Cornplanter, the science of battle was beautiful but merciless.

Both sides urged their Indian allies on to greater savagery, and the red men responded eagerly to the encouragement. Nevertheless, many of the wisest Indian councillors warned that participating in the white man's civil war would bring destruction to the Indian nations. White reprisals for Indian "massacres" were at least as merciless as the attacks that inspired them. General John Sullivan was ordered by Washington to break the power of the Iroquois, who had been attacking the frontiers of Pennsylvania and New York, aided by vengeful Tory legions. Sullivan's men laid waste to many peaceful villages and slaughtered hundreds of Indian prisoners, adopting as their battle cry, "Civilization or death to all American savages."

The Iroquois never recovered their majestic position, nor did the British do anything to save their allies when the war was over. Neither the British nor the Rebel government showed any gratitude to the red soldiery that had helped fight the Revolution. The Indians of America were the losers no matter which side they favored.

The following song is one of the war chants of the Algonquian Indians, who were, for the most part, Rebel supporters. As is true in so many Indian songs, the repetition of the simple phrases and melodies build in power and send the warrior into battle in a flame of intensity. To help the non-Indian singer, I have improvised English verses.

# Indian War Song

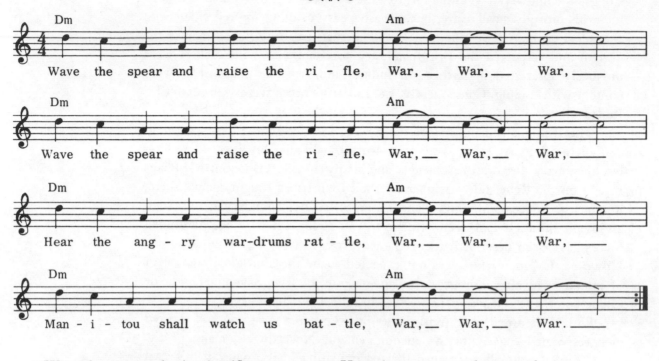

Wave the spear and raise the ri - fle, War,—— War,—— War,——

Wave the spear and raise the ri - fle, War,—— War,—— War,——

Hear the ang - ry war-drums rat - tle, War,—— War,—— War,——

Man - i - tou shall watch us bat - tle, War,—— War,—— War.——

Wave the spear and raise the rifle,
War, War, War,
Wave the spear and raise the rifle,
War, War, War.

Hear the angry war drums rattle,
War, War, War,
Manitou shall watch us battle,
War, War, War.

*Indian Warriors*

New music and edited text © 1972 by Oscar Brand

IN THE EARLIEST days of the Revolution, Washington organized a tiny navy which, during his siege of Boston, captured more than a score of British supply ships. The small store of supplies with which the General clothed his army came from captured naval stores. Then Congress voted to build thirteen new frigates in order to break the deadly British naval blockade. The captains assigned to the vessels were chosen for political rather than naval reasons, and they were of little use in the war. However, one of the ships which surrendered to a Royal warship after a stumbling defense became one of the British Navy's finest frigates, and helped destroy many of its sister ships.

There were a few exceptions to the general ineptitude which characterized official American naval exploits. In 1776, Captain Esek Hopkins led a small American squadron in a raid on Nassau in the West Indies. He brought back a shipload of supplies including badly needed munitions for the Rebel army.

Of the many frigates built by the Congress during the War, only one survived—the *Alliance*, of which sailors sang for many years,

> Though she, with her triumphant crew,
> Might to her fate all foes pursue,
> Yet, faithful to the land that bore,
> She stays, to guard her native shore.

Despite the rhyme, the *Alliance* did sail out and eventually joined John Paul Jones' marauding fleet later in the war.

But it was the great fleet of privateers that kept the British Navy from strangling the struggling young republic. In the first year of the war, these small, mercury-swift raiders captured nearly 300 British vessels. In the years which followed, no less than 1,697 privateers bedeviled the British, and these were manned by almost 58,000 American sailing men. It is estimated that this informal Navy, which was given official sanction by the receipt of letters of marque from the Congress, captured 600 British ships and at least $18,000,000 in supplies.

One of the most successful of the frigates funded by Congress was *The Providence*, commanded by Commodore Abraham Whipple. While cruising the Atlantic, she fell in with a convoy of 150 British ships escorted by a strong naval force. Taking advantage of a heavy fog, Whipple captured eleven ships and brought nine of them back to Boston. As was the custom, the captain and men split the proceeds with the Congress. Although the *Providence* was an official Navy frigate, the man who wrote the popular song about the exploit believed he was honoring her by referring to her as a "Yankee Privateer."

# The Yankee Privateer

Come lis - ten and I'll tell you how first I went to sea, — To
fight a - gainst the Bri - tish and win our lib - er - ty. We
shipped with Cap - tain Whip - ple who nev - er knew a fear, — The
Cap - tain of the *Prov - i - dence,* the Yan - kee pri - va - teer. *Chorus:* We
sailed and we sailed, and ___ kept ___ good ___ cheer, For
not a Bri - tish frig - ate could o'er - come the pri - va - teer.

Come listen, and I'll tell you how first I went
to sea,
To fight against the British and win our
liberty.
We shipped with Captain Whipple who never
knew a fear,
The Captain of the *Providence*, the Yankee
privateer.
CHORUS:
  We sailed and we sailed, and kept good
  cheer,
    For not a British frigate could o'ercome the
    privateer.

We sailed to the south'ard and suddenly did
meet,
Three British frigates—convoy to a West
Indian fleet,
Old Whipple put our lights out and crawled
upon their rear,
And not a soul suspected the Yankee privateer.
                                    CHORUS:

So slowly did we sail along, so silently we ran,
With no alarm we boarded the biggest mer-
chantman,
We knocked the watch down easily, the
lubbers shook for fear,
We took her prize without a shot for the
Yankee privateer.            CHORUS:

For ten long nights we followed and ere the
moon arose,
Each night a prize we captured beneath the
Lion's nose,
And when the British looked to see why ships
should disappear,
The found they had in convoy the Yankee
privateer.                    CHORUS:

The biggest British frigate bore round to give
us chase,
But though we were the fleeter, Old Whipple
didn't race,
Until he'd raked her fore and aft, for the
lubbers couldn't steer,
And then he showed the foe the heels of the
Yankee privateer.            CHORUS:

Then northward sailed our gallant ship to a
town that we all know,
And there we lay our prizes all anchored in
a row,
And welcome was our vict'ry to our friends
and fam'ly dear,
For we shared a million dollars on the Yankee
privateer.                    CHORUS:

New music and edited text © 1972 by Oscar Brand

---

JOHN PAUL JONES was born in Kircudbright, Scotland, in 1747.
Some historians claim that his father was the Earl of Selkirk. At the
age of twelve he became a sailor, at nineteen he was chief mate of a
slave ship, and at twenty-one he was captain of a trading vessel. At twenty-
six he settled in Virginia and adopted the Rebel cause. Sailing as a
Lieutenant under Commodore Esek Hopkins, he hoisted with his own
hands the first flag of an American squadron, a yellow-silk banner flaunting
a coiled rattlesnake, with the emblazoned warning, "Don't Tread On Me."

Assigned the command of a brigantine, he immediately demonstrated
his remarkable seamanship and his flamboyant courage by bringing in
sixteen captured vessels within four months. Fighting off British warships,
which had far superior armaments, he almost single-handedly ruined the
Nova Scotia fishing industry, a disaster which the British could hardly

afford. He once observed, "I do not wish to have command of any ship that does not sail fast, for I intend to go in harm's way." Throughout his brilliant career, his skill and daring made his inferior ships seem speedier than anything his opponents could muster.

Jones was assigned by Congress the command of the corvette, *The Ranger,* and immediately sailed across the Atlantic to bedevil the British in their home ports. In one of the most daring incidents of the war, possibly in memory of childhood slights, he led a raiding party ashore at St. Marys Isle where stood the Castle of the Earl of Selkirk. As one of his men reported, "Lord Selkirk was not at home and no man in the House. For the sake of his Lady and her Company they came off without doing any further Damage than plundering Him of Plate to the amount of 160 lbs of Silver." Later, Jones bought the plate from his men and sent it back to the Countess of Selkirk with his compliments.

The British people, fearful of invasion, demanded that the marauder be captured. Jones' answer was to destroy a pursuing sloop-of-war, *The Drake,* in a battle which lasted a little over an hour. Eager for a larger ship with which he could perform greater deeds, Jones got Benjamin Franklin to purchase an ancient, fat merchantship, which he called the *Bonhomme Richard* in honor of Franklin's famous publication, *Poor Richard's Almanac.* The ship was then fitted with forty cannon, some so decrepit that they exploded at the first discharge. It was with this inferior armament mounted on a rotten hulk that Jones fought one of the greatest seabattles of all time.

In 1779, in the North Sea, Jones sighted a British convoy of forty ships escorted by the 20-gun *Countess of Scarborough* and the 44-gun *Serapis.* Jones was accompanied by *The Pallas* and *The Alliance,* the latter commanded by Pierre Landais, a French naval officer in the American service. The *Pallas* engaged the *Countess of Scarborough,* while *The Richard* and *The Alliance* made for *The Serapis.* It was a bloody, terrible battle, during which *The Alliance,* for some strange reason, poured a number of deadly broadsides into *The Richard. The Richard* was already outgunned by the British, and had no need of punishment from an ally.

Captain Jones thereupon sailed his sinking ship to the side of the British vessel and lashed them together so that the broadsides were being fired almost muzzle to muzzle. After two bloody hours, Captain Pearson of *The Serapis* surrendered, and for his bravery was knighted by the King. When Jones heard of this later, he announced, "Should I fall in with him again, I'll make a lord of him."

The author of the song which follows is unknown, but it is found in numerous collections, both in Britain and the United States.

# An American Frigate

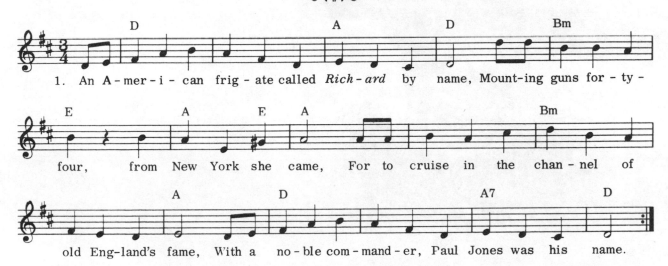

1. An A-mer-i-can frig-ate called *Rich-ard* by name, Mount-ing guns for-ty-four, from New York she came, For to cruise in the chan-nel of old Eng-land's fame, With a no-ble com-mand-er, Paul Jones was his name.

An American frigate called *Richard* by name,
Mounting guns forty-four, from New York she came,
For to cruise in the channel of old England's fame,
With a noble commander, Paul Jones was his name.

We had not sailed far when some ships we did spy,
A stout forty-four and a twenty likewise,
And forty bold shippen all laden with store,
And the convoy stood in for the old Yorkshire shore.

Paul Jones he did speak and to his men did say,
Let every man fight a good battle today,
We'll take that bold convoy in the height of her pride,
Or the *Richard* shall founder and sink in the tide.

The battle rolled on, until bold Pearson cried,
Have you yet struck your colors? Then come alongside.
But so far from thinking the battle was won,
Brave Paul Jones replied, I have not yet begun!

We fought them eight glasses, eight glasses so hot,
That seventy bold seamen lay dead on the spot,
And ninety brave seamen lay stretched in their gore,
While the pieces of cannon most fiercely did roar.

The *Alliance* bore down and the *Richard* did rake,
Which caused the bold hearts of our seamen to ache,
But the shot flew so hot that they couldn't stand it long,
And the brave British colors came finally down.

*John Paul Jones*

THE ENGLISH were tired of the war, and there was continuous objection in Parliament to its continuation. Besides, the dissidents declared, it's well-known that the American South is composed of large bodies of British sympathizers. Why not arm the American Tories and bring our Redcoats home? The new slogan for the day was, "Beat the Americans with Americans." Sir Henry Clinton was ordered to send over 3,000 troops to take Savannah, Georgia, and rally the southern Tories to the British flag. Having just been required to send 5,000 troops to protect the West Indies against the French, Clinton's northern army was thinning out. To one of his staff he complained, in tears, "I envy even that Grenadier who is passing the door, and would exchange with joy situations. No, let me advise you never to take command of an army."

Clinton was a conscientious soldier. With the aid of Major John André he overhauled his intelligence network. For the dangerous work of espionage he had plenty of Tory volunteers. He also set up fifteen regiments of Loyalist troops, including the Orange Rangers, the Roman Catholic Volunteers, the Volunteers of Ireland, the British Legion, and the Royal Americans Reformers. Next, Clinton decided to slow the movement of Rebel supplies from New England by taking over the Hudson River. With 6,000 picked troops ferried upriver, Stony Point Fort was taken—the first step toward capturing West Point.

[ 124 ]

While Clinton was fortifying Stony Point against an expected American attack, Washington sent Captain Allan McLane to spy out the British defenses. McLane was a hero and a veteran of many battles, but he dressed himself up as a backwoods militiaman and approached the British fortification in the company of a woman who was visiting her Redcoat sons. The British officers enjoyed making fun of the bumpkin and even showed him around the fort to watch his astonishment.

McLane reported back to Washington that the fortifications weren't as perfect as the British seemed to think, and described some of the more vulnerable approaches. For the attack, Washington turned to Anthony Wayne, hero of the Battle at Three Rivers, of Ticonderoga and Brandywine, of Germantown and Monmouth, who had earned his generalship in the Canadian campaign. He had so bedeviled the British with swift attacks and sudden withdrawals, that he had been named in admiration, "Mad Anthony."

Wayne ordered his men to unload their guns and fix bayonets, to ensure silence. Led by a friendly local black man, the Americans captured the outposts without a sound. Then the attack was made by two columns racing into the fort. In advance of the columns were "forlorn hopes"—ten men who plunged bravely into the midst of the enemy. Of the fifteen Americans killed in the battle, most were "forlorn hopes," but the British toll was 63 men killed and 553 taken prisoner. Anthony Wayne was wounded, but in twenty-five minutes Stony Point was taken.

As a gesture of gratitude Congress voted Wayne a gold medal. Then Washington decided to abandon Stony Point as difficult to defend. He had the cannon spiked and the fortifications broken down, then left the wrecked fort for the British to reenter. It may seem, today, like a fruitless victory, but it halted Clinton's march up the Hudson and lifted the spirits of a colonial people weary of civil warfare.

The following song, written by Wayne's aide de camp, is included in a number of Revolutionary War song collections.

# Anthony Wayne

His sword-blade gleams and his eye - light beams, And nev - er glanced ei-ther in vain; Like the o - cean tides at our head he rides, The fear - less Mad An - tho - ny Wayne. Bang! Bang! the ri - fles go, down falls the star - tled foe. *Chorus:* And man - y a red - coat here to - night, the Con - ti - nen - tals scorn - ing, Shall ne'er meet the blaze of the broad sun - light That shines on the mor - row morn - ing.——

His sword blade gleams and his eyelight
  beams,
And never glanced either in vain;
Like the ocean tides at our head he rides,
The fearless Mad Anthony Wayne.
Bang! Bang! the rifles go, down falls the
  startled foe.
CHORUS:
    And many a Redcoat here tonight, the
      Continentals scorning,
    Shall never meet the blaze of the broad
      sunlight
    That shines on the morrow morning.

Was e'er a chief of his speech so brief,
Who utters his wishes so plain?
Ere he speaks a word the orders are heard,
From the eyes of Mad Anthony Wayne.
Aim! Fire! exclaim his eyes; Bang! Bang! each
  gun replies,      CHORUS:

It is best to fall at our country's call,
If we must leave this lifetime of pain;
And who would shrink from the perilous
  brink,
When led by Mad Anthony Wayne?
Ran! Tan! the bugles sound, our forces fill
  the ground,      CHORUS:

Let them form their ranks in firm phalanx,
It will melt at our rifle-ball rain,
Every shot must tell on a Redcoat well,
Or we anger Mad Anthony Wayne.
Tramp! Tramp! away we go, now retreats
  the beaten foe,      CHORUS:

*Anthony Wayne storming Stony Point*

[ 127 ]

The seaborne forces which Clinton sent southward were successful in taking Savannah, Sunbury, and Augusta in Georgia. In this they were aided by the Tory sympathizers in the South, some of whom independently had been acting as a guerilla force, and had even bravely attacked a Rebel army of 2,000 men with one-third that number. Five of the Tories were hanged, and the Tory commander in Augusta retaliated by hanging a similar number of Whig prisoners. The passions inflamed by these acts of reciprocal inhumanity outlasted the war by many years.

By October 1779, nearly two-thirds of the British troops in Savannah were Loyalists. The situation was unendurable for southern Patriots. General Benjamin Lincoln of Massachusetts, who commanded the Rebel forces from his stronghold in Charleston, South Carolina, was urged to retrieve Savannah. Lincoln needed some sort of naval force and thought of the French Allied Fleet idling in the West Indies. A request for cooperation was sent and D'Estaing answered with dispatch, (which was the only action he ever took with proper speed, according to irate Rebel observers).

The Admiral began to unload his 6,000 French soldiers on September 12, 1779, then he paused to invite the British to surrender. He waited for a reply until October 9 and finally attacked in a joint pincer movement with General Lincoln's troops. By that time, the British had shored up their defenses and frightened the remaining Tories into joining their ranks. The combined attack was a combined failure. Lincoln demanded another assault, but D'Estaing had had enough of battle and proceeded to sail off again to the West Indies and less troubled waters.

The French lost in killed and wounded 637 men. The Americans lost 457. Among these was the Polish leader of cavalry, Casimir Pulaski, who had failed in a rebellion against Stanislaus, the King of Poland, and had fled with his followers to the New World. He was especially singled out for attack in the following Loyalist ballad (1779) because, like the French, he was intruding in a strictly British civil war.

# The Savannah Song

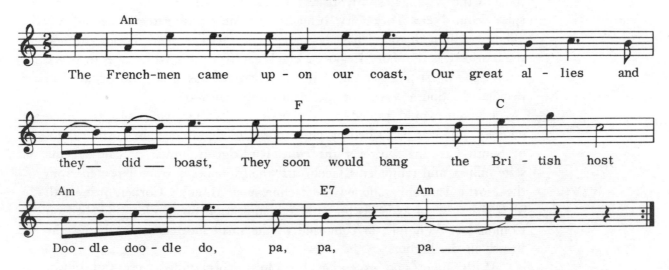

The French-men came up - on our coast, Our great al - lies and
they__ did__ boast, They soon would bang the Bri - tish host
Doo - dle doo - dle do, pa, pa, pa._____

The Frenchmen came upon the coast,
Our great allies, and they did boast,
They soon would bang the British host,
Doodle doodle do, pa, pa, pa.

D'Estaing he wrote to General Lincoln,
And told him that he need not think on,
Danger; but in quick step slink on,
Doodle doodle do, pa, pa, pa.

So Lincoln came down to Savannah,
The French and we all sung hosanna,
We soon will take them every man-a,
Doodle doodle do, pa, pa, pa.

But soon we found ourselves mistaken,
And were glad to save our bacon,
Rather than be killed or taken,
Doodle doodle do, pa, pa, pa.

The French, it's true, behaved quite civil,
Yet we wished them to the devil,
And hope that good may spring from evil,
Doodle doodle do, pa, pa, pa.

Pulaski fell, unworthy thing,
That once did try to kill his king,
With treason he'll make Hell to ring,
Doodle doodle do, pa, pa, pa.

And now that they on board have gone,
And left poor us here all alone,
We've nought to do but sigh and moan,
Doodle doodle do, pa, pa, pa.

The enemy doth keep their post,
Despite of all the Gallic host,
And Georgia we've forever lost,
Doodle doodle do, pa, pa, pa.

New music and edited text © 1972 by Oscar Brand

GENERAL LINCOLN, the Rebel general in the South, after the failure of his attack on Savannah, retreated to Charleston, determined to hold the city against any British attack. He had only 5,000 men, while spies from New York City brought the information that Clinton was sailing south with more than 8,000 regulars, Hessians, and Tories. Among the Tories was the Tory Legion, a crack cavalry outfit which was to prove one of the finest and fiercest of the attackers. It was 1780, and Britain had decided the South was to be the main theater of war.

Lincoln would probably have preferred withdrawing into the open country, but was persuaded by Governor Rutledge to remain in the capitol of South Carolina whatever the cost. Rutledge promised to call out the state militia, and reminded Lincoln that reinforcements were expected from the North. Lincoln stationed a detachment at Monck's Corner, just north of Charleston, to keep his lines of communication open. He also relied on Commodore Whipple, in command of the small local navy, to harass the British in the harbor.

With almost no exception Lincoln's expectations were unfulfilled. Commandor Whipple's ships found the harbor too shallow to maneuver in; the state militia came to the end of its enlistment time, and many went home to rest. The reinforcements under Baron De Kalb sent by Washington never arrived in Charleston. And the garrison that was supposed to keep open the line of retreat was wiped out by the Tory Legion. Meanwhile, the already large forces of Clinton were reinforced further by Lord Rawdon's 2,500 fresh troops sailing in from New York.

By May 12, 1780, Lincoln's situation was so hopeless that he had little alternative except to surrender his force of 5,000 men. With his men went a tremendous store of munitions and vital military supplies. It was the greatest single disaster suffered during the war by the Rebel forces. Except for the Governor, most of South Carolina's Rebel leaders were prisoners. Clinton was so pleased with his good fortune, that he set out on a spirited campaign, with uncharacteristic energy. The southern Tories were ecstatic, with visions of final victory dancing before their eyes, and infusing their newspapers and balladry.

# The Charleston Song

King Hancock sat in regal state,
And big with pride and vainly great,
Addressed his Rebel crew, addressed his Rebel
    crew:
"These haughty Britons soon shall yield
The boasted honors of the field,
While our brave sons pursue, while our brave
    sons pursue.

Six thousand fighting men or more,
Protect the Carolina shore,
And Freedom will defend, and Freedom will
    defend.
And stubborn Britons soon shall feel,
'Gainst Charleston and our hearts of steel,
How vainly they contend, how vainly they
    contend.

But ere he spoke, in dread array,
The Rebel foes, ill-fated day,
Saw British boys appear, saw British boys
    appear,

Their mien with martial ardor fired,
And by their country's wrongs inspired,
Shook Lincoln's heart with fear, shook Lincoln's
    heart with fear.

See Clinton brave, serene, and great,
For mighty deeds revered by fate,
Direct the thund'ring fight, direct the
    thund'ring fight,
While Mars, propitious God of war,
Looks down from his triumphal car,
With wonder and delight, with wonder and
    delight.

Our tars, their share of glories won,
For they among the bravest shone,
Undaunted, firm, and bold, undaunted, firm,
    and bold,
Whene'er engaged their ardor showed,
Their hearts with native valor glowed,
Hearts of British mold, of truest British mold.

New music and edited text © 1972 by Oscar Brand

[ 131 ]

*Major André*

THE BRITISH General Clinton's aide, Major John André, was effete, charming, and courageous. He had come to the colonies in 1774 as a lieutenant, and had been promoted in deserved recognition of his industry and bravery. He was also keenly interested in the theater and other lively arts, and wrote many lively and graceful songs and poems to amuse his friends.

But André's theatrical interests didn't prevent his organizing a valuable espionage system, using Tories and highly respected Rebel personalities in Rhode Island, Connecticut, New York, New Jersey, Pennsylvania, Maryland, Delaware, and New Hampshire. It is believed that one of his informants, probably a member of the Congress, was Samuel Chase, signer of the Declaration of Independence. Edward Bancroft, close friend and secretary to Benjamin Franklin, and adviser to the American delegation in France, was a British spy. Recently opened British intelligence papers refer discreetly to others in the British pay, many of whom probably retired after the war with honors befitting patriotic Rebels.

Major André recognized that many colonials had only a tenuous loyalty to the Revolution, and continually made tentative approaches to well-known Patriots. But his greatest catch was Benedict Arnold, who had saved the Revolution at least twice by his dedication and bravery. André had made a list of Rebel generals who might return to the Royal banner. Benedict Arnold's reputation was so firm that André hadn't even included him. Then strange messages began coming into British intelligence concerning a high Rebel officer who might, for a price, become a high Tory officer, André was astonished to learn that it was Major General Benedict Arnold. Furthermore, it was expected that Major General Arnold was going to be selected as commander of West Point—Clinton's dream of Hudson River conquest might finally come true.

While dealing with Arnold, André's poetic music didn't abandon him. He maintained his public image as a cavalier, and wrote a 61-verse epic called "The Cow Chase" celebrating Anthony Wayne's attack on Bull's Ferry just below Fort Lee on the Hudson. Washington had two reasons for ordering the assault. First, he hoped to take the British blockhouse, and second, he wanted some herds of cattle near the enemy lines driven into American hands for dining purposes.

These verses were published in the *Royal Gazette* after André was captured. The original copy has on it the following added stanza signed by the poet himself:

> When the epic strain was sung,
> The poet by the neck was hung,
> And to his cost he finds too late,
> The dung-born tribe decides his fate.

*Map of the scene of Arnold's treason*

# The Cow Chase

To drive the kine — one sum-mer's morn the tan-ner took — his way. — The calf shall rue — that is un-born the jum-bling of that day, — And Wayne de-scend-ing steers shall know and taunt-ing-ly de-ride, — And call to mind — in ev-'ry low the tan-ning of — his hide. —

To drive the kine one summer's morn the
tanner took his way.
The calf shall rue that is unborn the jumbling
of that day,
And Wayne-descending steers shall know and
tauntingly deride,
And call to mind in every low the tanning
of his hide.

All wondrous proud in arms they came, what
hero could refuse,
To tread the rugged path to fame—who had a
pair of shoes.
At six, the host with sweating buff arrived
at Freedom's pole,
And Wayne, who thought he'd time enough,
thus speechified the whole.

O ye, who glory doth unite, who Freedom's
cause espouse,
Whether the wing that's doomed to fight, or
that to drive the cows,
Their fort and blockhouse we will level and
deal a horrid slaughter,
We'll drive the scoundrels to the devil and
ravish wife and daughter.

And I, under cover of attack, whilst you are
all at blows,
From English neighborhood and Nyack will
drive away the cows,
For well you know the latter is the serious
operation,
And fighting with the refugees is only demon-
stration.

His daring words, from all the crowd such
    great applause did gain,
That every man declared aloud for serious
    work with Wayne,
And now the foe began to lead his forces to
    the attack,
Balls whistling unto balls succeed and make
    the blockhouse crack,

The firmer as the Rebels pressed, the loyal
    heroes stand,
Virtue had nerved each honest breast and
    industry each hand,
And as the fight was further fought and balls
    began to thicken,
The fray assumed, the generals thought, the
    color of a lickin'.

Yet undismayed the chiefs command, and to
    redeem the day,
Cry, "Soldiers, charge!" They hear, they stand,
    they turn and run away.
And now I've closed my epic strain, I tremble
    as I show it,
Lest this same warrior-drover, Wayne, should
    ever catch the poet.

*Anthony Wayne*

New music and edited text © 1972 by Oscar Brand

WHEN IN 1777 General Howe announced to his staff that he had been relieved of his command, the staff wept. Then Major André suggested giving the "old man" a going-away party, and nominated himself as the chief organizer and designer. It was to be a "Mischianza," from the Italian word meaning a tournament, and was to include dancing, fireworks, feasting, and gay theatricals. André planned all this while living in the house of Benjamin Franklin, and when finally the British were forced out of Philadelphia, André carried off with him as a souvenir a fine portrait of the wise old Rebel.

The Mischianza featured a pageant in which British officers in rainbow costumes portrayed "Knights of the Blended Rose" and "Knights of the Burning Mountain." André himself led the procession of the "Knights of the Blended Rose." Some of Philadelphia's leading beauties appeared in shimmering Turkish habiliments and scandalized the majority of proper Philadelphians. Among the Tory maidens invited to participate were the three beautiful daughters of wealthy Edward Shippen, Polly, Sally, and Peggy. Although it has been generally claimed that the three performed as requested, it's more likely that Mr. Shippen forbade the girls to appear in the immodest costumes designed by André.

Nevertheless, Peggy greatly admired the talent and grace of John André and even consented to sit for a lovely portrait which he drew of her, "Miss Margaret Shippen, daughter of Chief Justice Shippen." When the British left Philadelphia, Benedict Arnold took command of the city for the Rebel forces. Although one of the Revolution's greatest heroes, Arnold was continually under attack by the Congress for his careless financial dealings. He was always short of money—in part because he felt himself above such minor matters. Besides, Arnold was notoriously open-handed, and when he heard that General Joseph Warren's orphaned children were destitute while Congress argued over pensions, he hurriedly sent $500 to the family.

When he fell in love with Peggy Shippen, although she was, at eighteen, half his age, he resurrected some love letters he had sent unsuccessfully to another young lady only six months before, and announced, "Twenty times have I taken up my pen to write to you and as often has my trembling hand refused to obey the dictates of my heart." When they were married, he determined to keep her as expensively as had her wealthy father. But Congress kept preventing this. When charges were preferred against him and dismissed as unfounded, Congress disregarded its own committee and asked for a court-martial.

Peggy knew the young intelligence officer, André, very well, and it was probably for this reason that it was to André that Arnold sent his secret proposals. He would turn over the fortification plans for West Point and rally Tory strength around the British cause in return for 20,000 pounds—a tremendous sum in those days. André himself appeared at Arnold's headquarters and after agreeing to the bargain, left with the plans of West Point in his boot. On his way back to the British warship *The Vulture* waiting for him in the Hudson, he was stopped by a group of "volunteer militiamen" who, like privateers, were franchised to claim as a prize any property they might find on a captured enemy.

André could have shown them his pass from the unsuspected Arnold and have escaped without difficulty. After all, even if they were Loyalists, they would only have captured him and sent him to the very place he wished to be, British headquarters. Instead he committed the same mistake as had the amateur spy, Nathan Hale, and he announced to his surprised captors that he was a British officer. It's not known for sure whether they asked him for ransom, or whether he offered them a bribe, but after some dickering, their leader, John Paulding, took André to headquarters. John Jameson, the commander of the Rebel post decided to send a note to Washington and send the prisoner to his commander, Major General Benedict Arnold.

At that moment, Washington's manager of Secret-Service Activities, Major Benjamin Tallmadge, appeared on the scene. He dissuaded Jameson from remanding André to Arnold's care, but couldn't prevent him from informing Arnold of the capture. After all, Arnold was Jameson's commanding officer, and he could hardly take a chance that Arnold might be angry at a breach of military courtesy.

Arnold fled as soon as he heard the news of André's capture, leaving André in custody, the West Point plans on the way to General Washington. The abandoned Peggy Arnold thereupon enacted a theatrical tour de force of such power that she convinced the entire world, except for the few who knew better, that she had been deceived by her treacherous husband. As Alexander Hamilton wrote to his fiancée, "One moment she raved, another she melted into tears . . . It was the most affecting scene I was ever witness to." And so Peggy remained unpunished and Arnold went free. André was hanged.

I do not know who wrote the following ballad, but it is sung even today in the Hudson River Valley area.

# The Capture of Major Andre

Come all you brave Americans and unto me
    give ear,
I'll sing a little ditty that will your spirits
    cheer,
Concerning a young gentlemen whose age was
    twenty-two,
He fought for North America, his heart was
    just and true.

He with a scouting party went down to
    Tarrytown,
And met a British officer, a man of high
    reknown,
Who said unto brave Paulding, "You're of the
    British cheer,
I trust that you can tell me if there's any
    danger near."

Then up spoke this young hero, John Paulding
    was his name,
"Sir, tell us where you're going, and also
    whence you came?"
"I bear the British flag, sir, I've a pass to go
    this way,
I'm on an expedition, and have no time to stay."

Then round him came this company and bid
    him to dismount,
"Come tell us where you're going and give a
    strict account,
For we are now resolvéd that you shall ne'er
    pass by."
And when they had examined him they found
    he was a spy.

New music and edited text © 1972 by Oscar Brand

He beggéd for his liberty, he pled for his discharge,
And oftentimes he told them, if they'd set him at large,
"Here's all the gold and silver that I've laid up in store,
And when I reach the city I'll give you ten times more."

Then seeing his conspiracy would soon be brought to light,
He asked for pen and paper and begg'd for leave to write,
A line to General Arnold to let him know his fate,
To beg for his assistance, but alas, it was too late.

The news it came to Arnold and put him in a fret,
He walk'd the room in trouble till tears his cheek did wet,
The story soon would reach the camp of how he'd sold the Fort,
So he calléd for *The Vulture* and he sailéd for New York.

Now Arnold to New York has gone a-fighting for his King,
And left poor Major André on the gallows for to swing,
It moved each eye with pity, and caused each heart to bleed,
And everyone wished him released and Arnold in his stead.

A bumper to John Paulding and let your voices sound,
Fill up your flowing glasses and drink his health around,
And also to those gentlemen who bore him company,
Success to North America, ye sons of Liberty!

MOST OF Washington's leading generals were British-trained. Some of them were British-born. Some were British officers. By volunteering for colonial service they subjected themselves to charges of desertion and treason. For instance, the American general, Horatio Gates, the hero of Saratoga, was born in Essex, England. At an early age he joined the British Army and was assigned to duty in the thriving Canadian city of Halifax. He met George Washington when the Virginia militia accompanied General Braddock's ill-fated expedition during the French and Indian War.

Gates didn't think much of the Virginian, because, as a regular army officer, he despised the "Yankee Doodles" of the colonial militia, which was paid by local governments, often elected its own officers, and was known to resign from battle when faced by enemy forces. Nevertheless, as a bold volunteer in the Rebel forces, he was given special credit for having resigned his British commission.

Congress' infatuation with General Horatio Gates led to a costly blunder. Although Washington wanted Nathanael Greene to command the southern army, Gates was given the command. When Baron De Kalb, who had been fighting a holding action in North Carolina, heard Gates' plans, he was horrified. According to Gates, 7,000 experienced, well-equipped men would march through the night and attack the British under Lord Cornwallis. De Kalb tried to dissuade Gates, pointing out that the men were badly-equipped, hungry, inexperienced, and that there were actually less than 3,000 at the last muster. Gates cheerfully ignored the information and ordered the attack.

First, he sent Colonel Frances Marion's little band of guerrillas—"some white, some black," as someone put it—to cut British communications. They were fortunate, being thus spared from the terrible epidemic of diarrhea which spread through the camp. In the middle of the night, the weakened army ran headlong into the British forward units, for, by a remarkable coincidence, the British were mounting their own surprise night attack on the same road. Gates decided to fight right then and there. The American militia fled before the fury of the British assault and Gates fled with them, unaware that the regulars under De Kalb were holding steady. The British turned their entire attention to destroying De Kalb and decimating his command.

Gates was in disgrace, but he claimed one minor victory. A Tory regiment convoying American prisoners from the battlefield was suddenly smashed by a band of guerrillas which freed the prisoners and disappeared into the wilderness. The guerrillas were the same little band of irregulars, "some white, some black," who had been sent out under the command of Colonel Frances Marion. Cornwallis would always regret their escape.

Meanwhile, Washington wrote a letter to Gates, expressing his sympathy and his confidence in the beaten warrior. It was as if he were reassuring the old man, that militia or regular, victor or victim, the world would honor the volunteers who fought for independence. This song, voicing similar sentiments, was written by Henry Archer, of whom it was reported in 1778, "Philadelphia—Friday last, arrived in this city, Henry Archer, Esq. This young gentleman has been educated at a military school in England, where he owned a handsome fortune, which he has lately sold in order to embark as a volunteer in the American Army."

# The Bold Volunteer

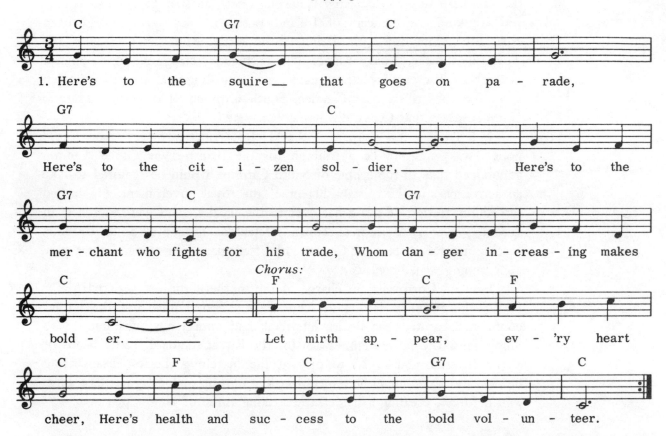

1. Here's to the squire __ that goes on pa - rade,
Here's to the cit - i - zen sol - dier, _____ Here's to the
mer - chant who fights for his trade, Whom dan - ger in - creas - ing makes
bold - er. _____ *Chorus:* Let mirth ap - pear, ev - 'ry heart
cheer, Here's health and suc - cess to the bold vol - un - teer.

Here's to the squire that goes on parade,
Here's to the citizen soldier,
Here's to the merchant who fights for his trade,
Whom danger increasing makes bolder.
CHORUS:
   Let mirth appear, ev'ry heart cheer,
   Here's health and success to the bold volun-
      teer.

Here's to the lawyer, who leaving the bar,
Hastens where honor doth lead, sir,
Changing his gown for the ensign of war,
The cause of his country to plead, sir. CHORUS:

Here's to the farmer who dares to advance,
To harvests of honor, with pleasure,
Who, bravely, with danger, will venture a
   chance,
A sword for his country to measure. CHORUS:

Here's to the soldier, though battered in wars,
And safe to his farmhouse retired,
When called by his country, ne'er thinks of his
   scars,
With ardor to join us inspired.    CHORUS:

Here's to the peer, first in senate and field,
Whose actions to titles add grace, sir,
Whose spirit undaunted would never yet yield,
To a foe, to a pension or place, sir, CHORUS:

THE VICTORY of the British at Camden was considered a special cause for Tory rejoicing. Nearly 2,400 Loyalist refugees were among the vanguard that had defeated Gates. Colonel Banastre Tarleton's cavalry, and Rawdon's Volunteers of Ireland—raised in Pennsylvania—had been especially distinguished for daring in the battle. Rivington's *Gazette*, the Tory mouthpiece, printed a mock advertisement offering millions of pounds as a reward for "a whole army, horse, foot, and dragoons, strayed or stolen from the subscriber, near Camden, South Carolina. The owner, Horatio Gates suspects that Cornwallis has stolen them."

It looked at this point as if the "Defeat Americans with Americans" policy was going to be a triumph for the British War Office. Clinton announced that all the people of South Carolina would be required to take an active part in the reestablishment of the royal government. He turned the administration of this order over to the Tories, who were merciless in avenging their own past mistreatment. Detachments scoured South Carolina forcing neutrals to take the Crown oath of allegiance, bringing about a state approaching armed civil war.

General Cornwallis, in charge of the southern theater, ordered Major Patrick Ferguson to lead a detachment of 1,000 Tories into the border country, to protect the British left flank and punish any inhabitants who didn't show the proper enthusiasm for the Royal standard. Little bands of angry frontiersmen began to pick at the marching Tories, disappearing before any action could be joined. Finally, a group of local guerrilla leaders joined forces, creating a fierce little striking force of almost 900 men.

*Lord Cornwallis*

*General Marion*

Ferguson was aware of some sort of threat, but had little information of its exact nature, since his scouts and outriders were continually being picked off by invisible enemies. Nor could he communicate with Cornwallis' headquarters for the same frightening reason. He decided to encamp atop King's Mountain, which was not far from the North Carolina border, and challenged "God Almighty and all the rebels outside of Hell." When the attack came it must have seemed to the entrenched Loyalists as if the challenge was being taken up by the exact number of Rebels addressed. For, in short time, Ferguson was killed and the entire detachment killed or captured.

Cornwallis began to realize the danger he was in. He withdrew south to Winnsboro, where he hoped his forces would be safe from the devastating strikes of the irregulars. But it was no use—Colonel Isaac Shelby, Colonel John Sevier, Colonel William Campbell, Colonel Benjamin Cleveland, General Thomas Sumter, General Andrew Pickens, and General Frances Marion snapped murderously at Cornwallis' troops until he wearily cursed "these plagues."

Possibly the most skillful of all was Marion, "The Swamp Fox." His base of operations seemed to be in the muddy wasteland between the Black and Pedee rivers, but Cornwallis' frequent searches never found their quarry. When Marion wished, he would crash out of the swamps with his hard-riding frontiersmen, sometimes up to the very gates of Charleston, and leave a path of devastation worthy of a marauding army instead of a few Rebel roughnecks. Swiftly returning to their hideaway, they would drink vinegar, swear mightily, and sing lustily through the misty nights.

# Marion's Men

We follow where the Swamp Fox guides,
His friends and merry men are we,
And when the Tory Legions ride
We burrow in the cypress trees.
The gloomy swampland is our bed,
Our home is in the red deer's den,
Our roof, the treetop overhead,
For we are wild and hunted men.
CHORUS:
    We ride, we hide, we strike again,
    For we are Marion's men.

We fly by day and shun its light,
But, prompt to strike the sudden blow,
We mount, and start with early night,
And through the forest track our foe,
And soon he hears our chargers leap,
And flashing saber blinds his eyes,
And ere he drives away his sleep,
And rushes from his camp, he dies.        CHORUS:

Now pile the brush and roll the log,
Hard pillow, but a soldier's head,
That's half the time in brake and bog,
Must never think of softer bed,
The owl is hooting to the night,
The cooter crawling o'er the bank,
And in that pond the plashing light,
Tells where the alligator sank.        CHORUS:

[ 144 ]

The Swamp Fox whistles to the scouts,
You hear his order calm and low,
Come, wave your torch across the dark,
We shall not be the last to go,
Have courage, comrades, Marion leads,
The Swamp Fox takes us out tonight,
So clear your swords and coax your steeds,
Tonight we ride, tonight we fight. CHORUS:

We follow where the Swamp Fox guides,
We leave the swamp and cypress tree,
Our spurs are in our coursers' sides,
And ready for the strife are we.
The Tory camp is now in sight,
And there he cowers within his den,
He hears our shout, he dreads the fight,
He fears, and flies from Marion's men. CHORUS:

*Colonel Tarleton*

"TARLETON'S QUARTER" was often the ferocious cry of the Rebels in the South, when they had overcome their enemy. It referred to the slaughter of Colonel Abraham Buford's Virginians by Tory cavalrymen under Lieutenant Colonel Banastre Tarleton in May 1780. Buford had asked for quarter when his men were surrounded, but Tarleton's men butchered the small group of regulars and militiamen, even putting the wounded to the sword. Every soldier under Gates' command fretted to even the score with the flamboyant young cavalry leader and his Tory followers.

The chance came when Washington convinced Congress to put Nathanael Greene in charge of southern operations. Greene was the son of a Quaker minister, but his devotion to the Revolution caused the Society of Friends to expel him in angry sorrow. He was the perfect man to take over the tangled and tortured affairs of the southern Rebels because, as Quartermaster General at Valley Forge, he was accustomed to "making do." When he discovered that he had only about 800 men fit for duty, with no provisions and no money to buy any, Greene must have faltered for a moment. Then he got busy "making do."

[ 145 ]

His first step was to take advantage of the skilled professional officers under his command. In particular, he gave huge Daniel Morgan 600 men to harass Cornwallis in the West. Splitting one's command in the face of a superior enemy force is against most tenets of military philosophy, but Greene felt the cruel, shifting southern war would allow the disregard of proper tactics. Cornwallis was genuinely puzzled by the maneuver, then sent out Banastre Tarleton and his Tory Legion, 1,000 men backed by strong reserves of British regulars.

On January 16, 1781, Morgan learned that Tarleton was galloping after him with a powerful force. He realized that a great part of his command was composed of local militia which often disappeared in the face of a superior enemy. Again controverting the usually immutable laws of battle, Morgan ordered the militia into the front lines, promising them that they would only be required to fire three volleys and then could retreat. "Three shots, boys, and you are free!"

Washington himself had said that no militia would "ever acquire the habits necessary to resist a regular force." As Tarleton's men advanced, their light cannon, called "grasshoppers," cut into the Rebel ranks, but the militia held. They discharged their promised three volleys, and then retired from the field with relief. They were met by Dan Morgan, who praised them mightily, formed them into columns and then, promising them glory and eternal gratitude, led them back into the fight. They were just in time, for Tarleton had almost rolled back the American line with his last reserves. The militiamen came around the flank and fired with devastating effect into the mass of Tarleton's troops. The British were torn apart and many tried to escape or surrender. Shouting, "Tarleton's Quarter!" the militia closed in. It was necessary for Morgan and his officers to order their troops back before they revenged themselves on the defeated Loyalists.

Tarleton and a few of his officers escaped from the conquering Rebels. The New Englanders in the ranks of the victors broke out with their favorite hymn, "Chester" (1778), a song by the earliest native-born composer in America, William Billings. So it was that the victory at Cowpens, so-called because the field of battle was at a grazing place called "Hannah's Cow Pens," was celebrated in South Carolina with a Massachusetts song.

# Chester

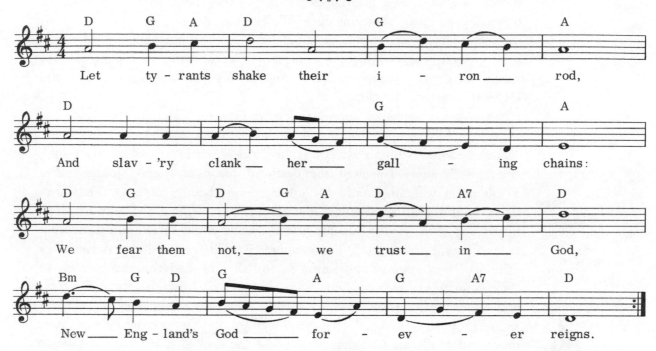

Let ty-rants shake their i - ron ___ rod,

And slav-'ry clank ___ her ___ gall - ing chains:

We fear them not, ___ we trust ___ in ___ God,

New ___ Eng-land's God ___ for - ev - er reigns.

Let tyrants shake their iron rod,
And slavery clank her galling chains:
We fear them not, we trust in God,
New England's God forever reigns.

Howe and Burgoyne, and Clinton, too,
With Prescott and Cornwallis join'd,
Together plot our overthrow,
In one infernal league combin'd.

When God inspired us for the fight,
Their ranks were broke, their lines were forced,
Their ships were shattered in our sight,
Or swiftly driven from our coast.

The foe comes on with haughty stride,
Our troops advance with martial noise,
Their veterans flee before our youth,
And gen'rals yield to beardless boys.

What grateful off'ring shall we bring?
What shall we render to the Lord?
Loud hallelujahs let us sing,
And praise his name on ev'ry chord.

IN MAY 1780, two Connecticut regiments struck for back pay. In January 1781, 2,400 Pennsylvanians mutinied and Congress agreed to redress the expressed grievances. A few weeks later three New Jersey regiments mutinied, but this time Washington decided to put a stop to the unmilitary behavior and executed some of the ringleaders on the spot. It is generally agreed that Washington ordered many men hanged, but would have been happy to have hanged only one—his former favorite, General Benedict Arnold.

Unofficial messages kept arriving at General Clinton's headquarters, after Arnold's escape, that a fair trade of André for Arnold might be arranged easily. Clinton always replied, "A deserter is never given up," although he truly lamented the death of his dear friend, John André. Washington wanted Arnold for other reasons besides revenge. His intelligence sources informed him that another Major-General had been involved in plotting with the British. He hoped that he could force the information from a recaptured Arnold. Furthermore, Arnold was issuing proclamations offering British money and uniforms to "all who had the real interest of their country at heart and who were determined to be no longer the tools and dupes of Congress." Arnold further called up the specter of religious warfare by announcing, "The eye which guides this pen lately saw your mean and profligate Congress at mass for the soul of a Roman Catholic in Purgatory."

*British grenadier*

Washington hastily called upon Sergeant Major John Champe, a 23-year-old Virginian, to kidnap Arnold from his New York stronghold. Champe, according to plan, raced out of camp, playing the role of a deserter. He was almost caught by an alert sentry, but managed to "escape" to the British lines, under the fire of his own angry colleagues. It was a very convincing performance, especially since he was almost killed. Brought directly to Sir Henry Clinton, the "deserter" announced that his comrades were discontented and that, "if the temper was properly cherished, Washington's ranks would not only be greatly thinned, but that some of his best corps would leave him."

Champe was personally urged by Arnold himself to join the new Tory Legion, and allowed himself to be persuaded. Then he informed his local espionage contact that he was ready. Washington sent back word that he wanted Arnold alive, and the kidnapping plot was set in motion. But when the cavalry attachment, which was to convey Arnold to General Washington, arrived at its appointed destination, neither Arnold nor Champe appeared. By coincidence, that very evening the new Tory legion and its newest recruit were ordered aboard a British warship to join the war in the south. Champe managed to escape when the legion joined Cornwallis in Virginia, and his story inspired some Revolutionary ballad-writer into creating a ballad in his honor.

*American Major-General*

# The Ballad of Sergeant Champe

Come, sheathe your swords, my gal-lant men, And lis-ten to the sto-ry, How Ser-geant Champe, one gloom-y night, Set out to catch the To-ry. For Gen-'ral Wash-ing-ton was mad, To think his plans had fal-tered, And swore by all, both good and bad, That Ar-nold should be hal-tered.

Come sheathe your swords, my gallant men,
And listen to the story,
How Sergeant Champe, one gloomy night,
Set out to catch the Tory.
For General Washington was mad,
To think his plans had faltered,
And swore by all, both good and bad,
That Arnold should be haltered.

He found a sergeant in his camp
Well made, of bone and muscle,
'Twas Sergeant Champe, who had many a year,
With Tories learned to tussle,
He boldly mounted on his horse,
All buttoned 'gainst the weather,
Sang out "Good-bye," and cracked his whip,
And soon was on the heather.

He galloped on toward Paulus Hook,
Improving every instant,
When suddenly a sharp patrol,
Espied him, very distant,
Then forty troopers, more or less,
To catch him did endeavor,
But just as they were at his heel,
He dived into the River.

And so it happened that brave Champe
Unto Sir Hal deserted,
Deceiving him, and you, and me,
And to New York was skirted.
He saw base Arnold in his camp,
Surrounded by his legion,
And told him the merry chase,
That brought him to that region.

New music and edited text © 1972 by Oscar Brand

Then Arnold grinned and rubbed his hands,
And almost choked with pleasure,
Not thinking Champe was all the while,
A-taking of his measure.

Come now, says he, my bold young man,
As you're within our borders,
Let's drink our fill, old care to kill,
Tomorrow you'll have orders.
But soon the British fleet set sail,
And wasn't that a pity?
For thus it was the plot was foiled,
And Champe sent from the city.

To southern climes the shipping flew,
To anchor in Virginny,
Then Champe escaped and joined his friends,
And back to home did shinny,
Base Arnold's head, by luck was saved,
Poor André then was gibbeted,
Arnold's to blame for André's fame,
And André's to be pitied.

*Musket called "Brown Bess"*

THE WAR had become even more bloody, bewildering, and bothersome. It was like some monstrous pet that violates the household with every stumbling move. Arnold's Tory Legions, with ferocious anger, raided the hapless settlements of Virginia, burning and killing wherever they suspected Rebel sympathies. Cornwallis was pursuing Greene and being mauled with each British victory. At Guilford Court House in North Carolina, Cornwallis was forced to fire grapeshot into his own troops, in order to drive back the Rebels with whom they were struggling. Charles Fox in the House of Commons, observed, "Another such victory would destroy the British Army." Greene's ragged men held together in the semblance of an army, even as Washington's weary soldiers had stayed intact at Valley Forge. Greene wrote, "We fight, get beat, rise and fight again."

[ 151 ]

Cornwallis called for reinforcements, but none were forthcoming. Spain had joined the allied forces against Britain, and the British Government was even more afraid of an invasion than before. Clinton was fearful of releasing any troops for the southern theater because of reports that Washington and Rochambeau were planning to attack New York. In reality, his intelligence sources were being fed this information by "deserters" and "Tories" working under Washington's direction. The Commander-in-Chief was one of the cagiest officers ever to take the field in battle. An admiring Frenchman declared that Washington was the prince of deceivers and that no one could tell the size of his army from one moment to another. When there were few men, Washington spread them about the camp, when there were many he had them crowd into tiny tents. He had nightfires lit in numbers suitable for armies when there were only a few regiments in the field. British intelligence was puzzled.

Despite his obvious preparations for an attack on New York, Washington had decided to move south. Admiral de Grasse, who had taken over from D'Estaing, informed Washington that he could bring 29 ships and three new French regiments to Chesapeake Bay. There Cornwallis was encamped near Yorktown, Virginia, after having vainly chased Lafayette about the colony. Cornwallis might have escaped the trap that was being sprung, but he relied on information brought him by another "deserter," Private Charles Morgan. Morgan, questioned by Cornwallis and Banastre Tarleton, warned that Lafayette had a fleet of boats capable of carrying his entire force, which would enable him to cut off a British movement toward the north.

To deceive Clinton into further thinking that New York would be the point of Rebel attack, Washington ordered his entire French-American force to halt in New Jersey and build a permanent camp, including five tremendous ovens. The tall Virginian, coming "by coincidence upon a known Tory informer, asked naive questions about beaches on Long Island and Sandy Hook. One German officer began to suspect the deception when he heard that a French officer had shipped his mistress south. But the flood of information coming into British headquarters seemed to point to a combined attack in the north.

The British realized the truth weeks later when a report came from Philadelphia that Washington and his troops had marched through on the way to Virginia. The swift-moving colonial troops hoped that the great battle they were soon to engage in would fulfill the promise of a song recently written by a New York soldier.

# Fare Thee Well, You Sweethearts

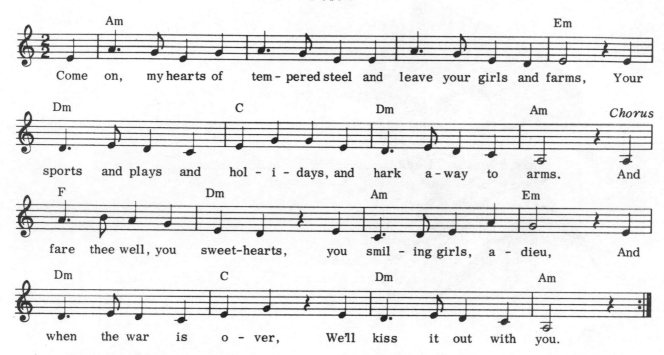

Come on, my hearts of tem-pered steel and leave your girls and farms, Your
sports and plays and hol-i-days, and hark a-way to arms. And
fare thee well, you sweet-hearts, you smil-ing girls, a-dieu, And
when the war is o-ver, We'll kiss it out with you.

Come on, my hearts of tempered steel and
    leave your girls and farms,
Your sports and plays and holidays, and hark
    away to arms.
CHORUS:
    And fare thee well, you sweethearts,
    You smiling girls, adieu,
    And when the war is over,
    We'll kiss it out with you.

No foreign slaves shall give us laws, no British
    tyrant reign,
'Tis Independence made us free and freedom
    we'll maintain,    CHORUS:

We'll charge the foe from post to post, attack
    their works and lines,
And by our well-laid stratagems we'll make
    them all Burgoynes.    CHORUS:

And when the war is over we will set us down
    at ease,
And plow and sow and reap and mow, and
    live just as we please,    CHORUS:

The rising world shall sing of us a thousand
    years to come,
And tell our children's children of the wonders
    we have done,    CHORUS:

And then each lad shall take his lass all beaming
    like a star,
And in her loving arms forget the dangers of
    the war,    CHORUS:

New music and edited text © 1972 by Oscar Brand

[ 153 ]

*Rochambeau*

WHILE WASHINGTON was preparing for his surprise move to
the south, Lafayette was maneuvering in Virginia with three regiments of light infantry. Historians have suggested that the Marquis had been sent south by Washington as a result of the Chief's obsession with Benedict Arnold. Arnold was in Virginia, and Washington wanted his head. Four attempts to kidnap Arnold had failed—perhaps the old warrior couldn't be taken except on the field of battle. If this was Washington's sole reason for sending Lafayette south, it was in vain. Arnold was to die in England years later, sad but unrepentant.

Nevertheless, Lafayette's expedition was a very valuable one. His men learned to break camp hurriedly at the approach of the superior British force, and to work hand in hand with irregular forces which would appear out of swamps and woodlands as they retreated by. With only 3,000 men, many of them militia, Lafayette knew better than to engage Cornwallis in battle. He wrote to Washington, "I am not strong enough even to get beaten."

As the warring armies trampled across Virginia, civil war followed the devastation they left behind. Estates and property changed hands over and over, and murder and robbery were accepted as political events. It was pointed out in a Tory journal that any act was condoned if the victim had been mistaken for a Loyalist, and was altogether excused if the victim could be proved to have been a Tory sympathizer.

Everyone was raiding everyone else. Colonel Banastre Tarleton, with a fierce little striking force of British dragoons, raided Charlottesville, the capitol of Virginia, and almost came away with Thomas Jefferson. When Jefferson fled, Tarleton captured a couple of state legislators instead.

To add to the confusion more columns of troops came down from the North, some commanded by Anthony Wayne, others by Baron Von Steuben. Cornwallis began to edge toward the sea, where, in the past, the British Navy had always been waiting. But this time only a few ships were in evidence. Clinton, still sure that Washington meant to attack New York, was holding tight to the major portion of the fleet. As a matter of fact, he requested Cornwallis to send 3,000 of his soldiers back to New York.

Obediently, Cornwallis ordered 3,000 sorely needed troops to prepare to embark for New York. At that moment a new dispatch arrived cancelling the first request. This was followed by another dispatch countermanding the second dispatch. Cornwallis settled his men in Yorktown, Virginia, weary after months of such intricate maneuvers that historians still find it difficult to map the Southern campaign. When the French under Rochambeau and Admiral De Grasse appeared, and Washington finally revealed that he was committed to a southern attack, ballad-makers wrote about Cornwallis and his army as if they had been engaged in some kind of comic choreography.

*Remains of the Entrenchments at Yorktown*

# The Cornwallis Country Dance

Cornwallis led a country dance, the like was never seen, sir,
Much retrograde and much advance and all with General Greene, sir.
They rambled up and rambled down, joined hands and then they run, sir,
Our General Greene to Charlestown and the Earl to Wilmington, sir.

Cornwallis led a country dance, the like was
    never seen, sir,
Much retrograde and much advance and all
    with General Greene, sir.
They rambled up and rambled down, joined
    hands and then they run, sir,
Our General Greene to Charlestown and the
    Earl to Wilmington, sir.

Greene in the South then danced a set and got
    a mighty name, sir,
Cornwallis jigged with Lafayette but suffered
    in his fame, sir,
Quoth he, "My guards are weary grown with
    footing country dances.
They never at St. James's shone at capers, kicks,
    and prances."

"Though men so gallant ne'er were seen while
    sauntering on parade, sir,
Or wriggling o'er the Park's smooth green or
    at a masquerade, sir,
Yet are red heels and long-laced skirts for
    stumps and briars meet, sir,
Or stand they chance with hunting-shirts, or
    hardy veteran feet, sir?"

Now housed in York he challenged all to minu-
    ets so sprightly,
And lessons for a courtly ball his soldiers
    studied nightly,
His challenge heard, full soon there came a set
    who knew the dance, sir,
De Grasse and Rochambeau, whose fame proved
    certain to advance, sir.

[ 156 ]

And Washington, Columbia's son, whom easy nature taught, sir,
That grace which can't by pains be won, nor monarch's gold be bought, sir,
Now hand in hand they circle round, this ever-dancing peer, sir,
Their gentle movements soon confound the Earl, as they draw near, sir.

His music he forgets to play, his feet can move no more, sir,
And all his soldiers curse the day they jiggled to our shore, sir,
Now, Tories all, what will you say? Come, is this not a griper?
That while your hopes are danced away, 'tis you must pay the piper.

*Cornwallis' surrender*

THE BRITISH counted heavily on their naval supremacy. But when Spain joined the war in 1779—although only as an ally of France, not of the colonies—the British fleet was forced to disperse its strength throughout the Empire. Holland, too, was a declared enemy of the Crown, though by inadvertence. This had come about when an American packet was captured by a British cruiser and the American minister to the Netherlands, Henry Laurens, tried to dump his political papers into the sea. Among these was a proposal for a "model treaty" with Holland. The English government believed it to be a genuine document, and hastily instructed Admiral George Brydges Rodney, to attack the Dutch island of St. Eustatius before the Dutch in the West Indies learned of the declaration of war.

This high-handed act was typical, according to neutral nations, of Britain's reprehensible maritime policy. Led by Catherine II of Russia, the neutrals formed "The League of Armed Neutrality," which was dedicated to the breaking of England's naval blockade. Yet, despite this whittling down of Britain's naval strength, Washington knew there was little time left for his grand plan. French Admiral De Grasse had informed him that half his ships had been ordered home and that he could postpone his departure for only a few more days.

Nearly 9,000 American troops and 8,000 French were arriving at Yorktown. Cornwallis was prevented from escaping by the French Fleet and its disembarked soldiers. And then the British fleet appeared, commanded by Admiral Thomas Graves. They engaged, cannonaded, maneuvered, disengaged, and withdrew to take each others' measure once again. Then an additional French complement of ships arrived bringing the French strength to 36 ships of the line to the British 19. Graves decided to preserve the Navy at the expense of Cornwallis' beleaguered army, and sailed back to New York to report his misadventures to Sir Henry Clinton.

Cornwallis had been deceived as completely as Clinton. Believing that the joint attack would thrust at New York, he had offered to send at least a thousand men to Clinton's aid. Now he knew how dangerous his position was. In happier days he had argued against the war so vehemently that he had been forced to withdraw from the House of Lords. Now he and his army would be the victims of other men's follies. As the siege guns began to pound his vulnerable positions, Cornwallis wrote to Clinton, "The safety of the place is . . . so precarious that I cannot recommend that the fleet and the army should run great risque in endeavouring to save us." On October 19, 1781, Cornwallis surrendered his entire army to the combined forces of Washington and Rochambeau.

According to New Englander Lemuel Cook, "Washington ordered that there should be no laughing at the British; said it was bad enough to have to surrender without being insulted." Dr. James Thacher, a surgeon in the American infantry, reported, "Their mortification could not be concealed . . . many of the soldiers manifested a sullen temper, throwing their arms on the pile with violence, as if determined to render them useless." It has been chronicled that the fife-and-drum corps struck up the melody of "The World Turned Upside Down." It was certainly an appropriate theme for the occasion.

# The World Turned Upside Down

If buttercups buzzed after the bee,
If boats were on land and churches on sea,
If ponies rode men,
And if grass ate the cows,
If cats should be chased into holes by the
   mouse,
If the mammas sold their babies to the gypsies
   for half a crown,
If summer were spring, and the other way
   'round,
Then all the world would be upside down.

CORNWALLIS SURRENDERED on October 19, 1781, delivering an army of 7,000 seasoned veterans to the Rebels as prisoners. On that same day, 35 ships set sail from New York to relieve the siege of Yorktown, carrying 7,000 of Clinton's best troops. When the rescue fleet arrived on the 24th, Clinton was informed of the disaster, and returned in mortification to New York. It was generally believed that the war would now wind down swiftly.

Negotiations dragged on for years. The war on the American mainland dwindled down to meaningless skirmishes and random volleys, but the seas were alive with privateers and warships. During six months of 1782, Captain Joseph Robinson's *Pilgrim* out of Salem took more than 25 prizes in the Atlantic and Caribbean. On the day the news arrived that a peace treaty had been finally signed, French and British warships were engaged in battle off the coast of India.

Benjamin Franklin refused to negotiate major questions until he could arrange for the release of American naval prisoners held by the British. This required a special act of Parliament because these sailors were being held as Rebels and pirates, rather than prisoners of war.

The sea war was fought, too, off the West Indies where, in 1782, Admiral Rodney's ships captured five French vessels, including Admiral De Grasse's 110-gun flagship *Ville de Paris*. The Spanish fleet tried to take Gibraltar that same year, but a battered English convoy arrived just in time to rescue the "Rock."

By 1782 the war was winding down, and changes in both Britain and America were necessary to accommodate the new nation, still the home of many Tories, and the mother nation, almost wholly defeated and discredited. Lord North was deposed so that the American Commissioners John Jay, John Adams, Henry Laurens, and Benjamin Franklin, could treat with the Marquis of Rockingham, who had always opposed the war. George III talked miserably of retiring to Hanover, but yielded to unenthusiastic persuasion. American merchants, many of whom had supported the war in the hope of cancelling their debts to British interests, learned to their chagrin that they would have to pay Britain after all. British merchants, fearful that their trading with the enemy would be punished, were relieved when captured documents proving their guilt were quietly buried in the government's "dead secret" files.

In New York, the Tories understood full well that they must soon be on their way. The newspapers began to be filled with offers of property for sale. "Genteel furniture" was advertised at a great discount. The King offered to transport to Canada all loyal subjects who had lived within the British line for at least twelve months. Agents were sent to report on the prospects of living in Nova Scotia. The following song, printed in the *Brooklyne-Hall Super Extra Gazette* of June 8, 1782, demonstrates that the Tories regretted only the loss of the war, but never their loyalty to the King.

# Unhappy Times

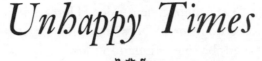

Un - hap - py times ___ of late we've seen, Un - hap - py days in - deed, ___ For such the rue - ful hours have been, Did make ___ our hearts to bleed. ___

Unhappy times of late we've seen,
Unhappy days indeed,
For such the rueful hours have been,
Did make our hearts to bleed.

Rebellion did with all its force,
Pour down upon our heads,
The stream took such a rapid course,
It drove us from our beds.

But still the King's loyal army stands,
And peace must be their choice,
That such disasters be no more,
With one accord rejoice.

For glorious news surround our King,
And England's noble cause,
So all true souls and faithful men,
Will shout with one applause.

For now with safety we may keep,
Our hard-begotten shore,
For insecurity we sleep,
And bury gold no more.

No more our flocks and herds will stray,
Our nymphs and swains shall sing,
And ever bless the welcome day,
That binds us to our King.

New music and edited text © 1972 by Oscar Brand

J AMES RIVINGTON, the printer who had inspired the Tories through- out the Revolution with his broadsides, songs, poems, and satirical re- ports, announced in anticipation of Rebel revenge that he was "sensible that his zeal for the success of his Majesty's Arms, his sanguine wishes for the good of his country, and his friendship for individuals, had at times led him to credit and circulate paragraphs without investigating the facts so closely as his duty to the public demanded. Hereafter he would err no more."

The Rebels outside of New York hooted at this token conversion. One critic proposed boiling Rivington down into soup to be fed to Tories bound for England. In December of 1782, Rivington printed a further ex- planation of his behavior, calling it "Reflections." He even stayed to print his *Gazette* after the Whips returned to New York, but he was finally forced to leave as a result of public displeasure.

Perhaps one should read the following "Reflections" now, before reading further on this page. After examining and analyzing the noted Tory's words, one might then read the next paragraph on this page and then look the song over again, remembering that the man who wrote it was a hard-core Loyalist who tried to pacify the victorious Rebels but failed dismally.

Many of the Tory songs in this collection owe their survival to the fact that Rivington printed them. It is possible that he wrote some of them. It is also amazing that he found the time to edit a newspaper at all, since he was busy with many other pursuits. In fact, in 1959 it was discovered that Rivington was one of George Washington's most efficient spies. He is credited with the remarkable feat of stealing the British Navy signal book, which American headquarters turned over to Admiral De Grasse.

How many other Tories were secret Rebel agents and how many Rebels were secret Tories may never be known. Perhaps it is not even important. But Canada surely profited by the immigration of almost 100,000 Loyalists while the new American republic lost some of its most valuable citizens. In a country of only two and a half million, 100,000 emigrants left a melancholy void.

# Rivington's Reflections

The more I reflect, the more plain it appears,
If I stay, I must stay at the risk of my ears.
I have so be-peppered the foes of our throne,
Be-rebeled, be-deviled, and told them their own,
That if we give up to these Rebels at last,
'Tis a chance if my ears will atone for the past.

Yet still I surmise that for aught I can see,
No Congress or Senates would meddle with me,
For what have I done, when we come to con-
    sider,
But sold my commodities to the best bidder,
If I offered to lie for the sake of a post,
Was I to be blamed if the King offered most?

Around me all swear as a very last shift,
They will go to New Scotland and take the
    King's gift,
Good folks do your will, but I vow and I
    swear,
I'll be boiled into soup before I will live there,
Of all the vile countries that ever were known,
It's the worst in the torrid or temperate zone.

Shall I push for old England and whine at the
    throne?
Alas, they have Jemmies enough of their own,
Besides, such a name I have got from my trade,
They would think I was lying whatever I said,
In short, if they let me remain in this realm,
What matters it to me who stands at the helm.

New music and edited text © 1972 by Oscar Brand

THE TREATY that the Commissioners hammered out with England was illegal in that Congress had promised the French not to treat unilaterally with the British government. But the Americans knew that France was not a friend to democracy and that her ally, Spain, was, in fact, hostile toward American independence. Once the basic agreement was worked out, the French and Spanish rushed in to stake their claims.

Franklin had demanded the whole province of Canada, but Shelburne, negotiating for England, balked at this outrageous effrontery. Instead, after months of secret negotiation, it was agreed to draw a northern frontier from the borders of Maine to the St. Lawrence River and through the Great Lakes. Everything south of the frontier, east of the Mississippi, and north of Florida became American territory. The British negotiator knew he would be attacked by the powerful interests that financed the Canadian fur companies, but he had little choice in the matter.

For the New England states, the Commissioners demanded and were promised fishing rights off the coast of Newfoundland. Congress, in turn, promised to use its good offices to arrange for payments of the debts owed by its citizens to creditors in England and to compensate the Loyalists for loss of property. The Commissioners agreed to this, well knowing that good offices are often unavailing.

When France's turn came to claw out a few pieces of the British Empire, she was given the island of Tobago, recognition of fishing rights off Newfoundland, rights to her possessions in India and the West Indies, and some slave-trade settlements on the African coast. Spain managed to hold on to Minorca, which she had taken during the war, and acquired the two English colonies in East Florida.

The War and its aftermath shook the British system to its foundations. William Pitt, the Earl of Chatham's son, was acclaimed Prime Minister. Reformers demanded an end to the slave trade, but Pitt insisted on moving slowly. Finally, his government fell, and it was left to his rival, Charles Fox, to end slavery in England. In America, a compromise with the South maintained the institution of slavery for almost a century. Many American blacks who had fought in the Revolution left the country they had helped create to begin life anew in the land against which they had taken up arms.

The song "Good Bye to America" was printed on a broadside in England soon after the Revolution. "God Save Our States" was published in the *Pennsylvania Packet*, as "made by a Dutch lady at the Hague, for the sailors of the five American vessels at Amsterdam . . ."

# Good Bye to America

Now, farewell, my Massa, my Missy, adieu,
More blows and more stripes will I ne'er take
    from you,
Or "Will you come hither" and "Thither you
    go,"
Or help make you rich by the sweat of my
    brow.

Farewell the mosquito, farewell the black fly,
And rattlesnake, too, who may sting me to die,
This Negro go home to his old Galilee,
Before he consent to be nevermore free.

Den, hey, for old England, where liberty
    reigns,
Where Negroes ain't beaten and loaded with
    chains,
And if I return to the life that I had,
You can put me in chains, 'cause I surely be
    mad.

New music and edited text © 1972 by Oscar Brand

# God Save Our States

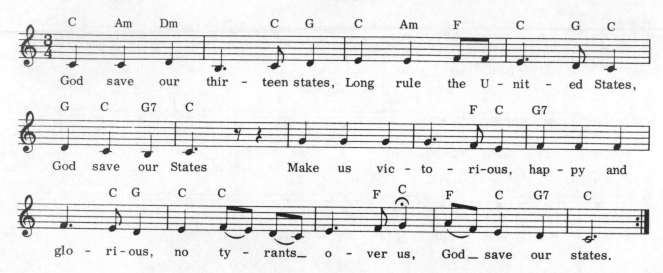

God save our thir - teen states, Long rule the U - nit - ed States, God save our States Make us vic - to - ri - ous, hap - py and glo - ri - ous, no ty - rants— o - ver us, God— save our states.

God save the thirteen States,
Long rule the United States,
God save our States.
Make us victorious, happy and glorious,
No tyrants over us,
God save our States.

Oft did Americay, forsee with sad dismay,
Her slavery near,
Oft did her grievance state, but Britain, falsely great,
Urging her desperate fate, turned a deaf ear.

Now the proud British foe we've made by victory know,
Our sacred right,
Witness at Bunker's Hill, where godlike Warren fell,
Happy his blood to spill in gallant fight.

To our famed Washington, brave Stark at Bennington,
Glory is due,
Peace to Montgomery's shade who, as he fought and bled,
Drew honors round his head, numerous as true.

Look to Sar'toga's plain, our captures on the main,
Moultrie's defense,
Our catalogue is long of heroes yet unsung,
Who noble feats have done for Independence.

We'll fear no tyrant's nod, nor stern oppression's rod,
Till Time's no more,
Thus Liberty, when driven from Europe's states, is given,
A safe retreat and haven on our free shore.

New music arrangement and edited text © 1972 by Oscar Brand

[ 166 ]

*Jefferson reading the Declaration of Independence*

# Index of Titles

# Index of First Lines

# Historical Index